Praise for *Conte...*

"The Web democratized access to publishing ... manual. I don't know anyone more qualified ... you aspire to be a competent publisher, peek insi... keep the great publishers on top."

—Ted McConnell, EVP Digital, Advertising Research Foundation (ARF)

"The massively experienced Rebecca Lieb is an engaging writer who gets right to the heart of creating content that attracts attention and turns readers and watchers into customers. This easy-to-read, how-to primer is a must-read for beginners who need a clue and old timers ready for a refresher. This book is crisp but not trivial, comprehensive but not ponderous, and useful but not pedantic. You should have bought it by now."

—Jim Sterne, eMetrics Marketing Optimization Summit
Founder and Web Analytics Association Chairman

"Content marketing is about optimizing the dialogue between a company and its customers for profitable outcomes. The better the conversation is, the more attention it attracts, and the more your customers are compelled to talk and buy. Almost any company or service can find a content marketing strategy that will work for it. And with an economic forecast that's challenging for at least the near future, it's easy to make a case for leveraging content for all it's worth. This book explains the nuts and bolts of content marketing, from developing a strategy to putting it into practice to measuring and improving results. If your business has any kind of a digital presence, from a website to a Facebook page or a Twitter account, you can't afford not to read it—now."

—Bryan Eisenberg, marketing speaker and co-author of *The Wall Street Journal*,
BusinessWeek, *USA Today*, and *The New York Times* bestselling books *Call to
Action*, *Waiting For Your Cat to Bark?*, and *Always Be Testing*.

"Content creation can be a tough task, but there's no one in this industry that understands the ins and outs of creating highly valuable and thoroughly optimized content like Rebecca Lieb. These days, it's not just about putting words up in a blog post, and Rebecca is one of the top authorities to teach marketers how to create content that resonates with their audiences, social communities, and search engines. If you're going to buy any book to teach you about creating valuable content for your audience, it should be this book!"

—Liana "Li" Evans, author of *Social Media Marketing:
Strategies for Engaging in Facebook, Twitter & Other Social Media*

"Many books on digital marketing are glorified blog posts—one good idea painfully stretched out over hundreds of pages. *Content Marketing* is something different; a rich and useful study of the new engine of marketing. Whether you sell locally or across the globe, you will come away with a new understanding of how to build a powerful content strategy and the tactics to make it work."

—Stefan Tornquist, VP Research for Econsultancy U.S.

"Content is king. Unless it's not. *Content Marketing* will ensure a brand's content is always kingly, always works towards increasing sales, and always reduces marketing costs."

—Steve Hall, Adrants, Editor

"Clearly reflecting Rebecca's deep digital publishing experience, this book provides step-by-step guidance on how to plan, produce, promote, and measure content marketing. Even more importantly, as it's often the greater challenge, it outlines how to integrate content marketing into other existing marketing functions such as advertising, social media, etc."

—Pauline Ores, Industry Principal, Infosys

CONTENT MARKETING

Think Like a Publisher—How to
Use Content to Market Online
and in Social Media

REBECCA LIEB

800 East 96th Street,
Indianapolis, Indiana 46240 USA

Content Marketing: Think Like a Publisher—How to Use Content to Market Online and in Social Media

ISBN-13: 978-0-7897-4837-9
ISBN-10: 0-7897-4837-1

Library of Congress Cataloging-in-Publication data is on file.

Printed in the United States of America

Second Printing: December 2011

Trademarks

Warning and Disclaimer

Bulk Sales

Que Publishing offers excellent discounts on this book when ordered in quantity for bulk purchases or special sales. For more information, please contact

U.S. Corporate and Government Sales
1-800-382-3419
corpsales@pearsontechgroup.com

For sales outside of the U.S., please contact

International Sales
international@pearson.com

Editor-in-Chief
Greg Wiegand

Acquisitions Editor
Rick Kughen

Development Editor
Rick Kughen

Managing Editor
Sandra Schroeder

Project Editor
Seth Kerney

Copy Editor
Gill Editorial Services

Indexer
Brad Herriman

Proofreader
Apostrophe Editing Services

Technical Editor
Sally Falkow

Publishing Coordinator
Cindy Teeters

Book Designer
Anne Jones

Compositor
Trina Wurst

CONTENTS AT A GLANCE

TABLE OF CONTENTS

PART III: GETTING TACTICAL: CONTENT NUTS & BOLTS

PART IV: IT'S NEVER OVER—POST-PUBLICATION

About the Author

 **Rebecca Lieb** is globally recognized as an expert on digital marketing, advertising, publishing, and media. A consultant, author, and sought-after speaker, she is Altimeter Group's digital advertising and media analyst. Earlier, Rebecca launched and ran Econsultancy's U.S. operations. She was VP and editor-in-chief of The ClickZ Network for more than seven years. For a portion of that time, Rebecca also ran Search Engine Watch. She consults on content strategy for a variety of brands and professional trade organizations. Earlier, Rebecca held executive marketing and communications positions at strategic eservices consultancies, including Siegel+Gale. She has worked in the same capacity for global entertainment and media companies including Universal Television & Networks Group (formerly USA Networks International) and Bertelsmann's RTL Television. As a journalist, Rebecca has written on media for numerous publications, including *The New York Times* and *The Wall Street Journal*. She spent five years as *Variety*'s Berlin-based German/Eastern European bureau chief. Until recently, Rebecca taught at New York University's Center for Publishing, where she also served on the Electronic Publishing Advisory Group.

Her first book, *The Truth About Search Engine Optimization*, published by FT Press, instantly became a best seller on Amazon.com. It remains a top-10 title in several Internet marketing categories.

Dedication

For rbrt, source of a great deal of contentment.

We Want to Hear from You!

As the reader of this book, *you* are our most important critic and commentator. We value your opinion and want to know what we're doing right, what we could do better, what areas you'd like to see us publish in, and any other words of wisdom you're willing to pass our way.

As an editor-in-chief for Que Publishing, I welcome your comments. You can email or write me directly to let me know what you did or didn't like about this book—as well as what we can do to make our books better.

Please note that I cannot help you with technical problems related to the topic of this book. We do have a User Services group, however, where I will forward specific technical questions related to the book.

When you write, please be sure to include this book's title and author as well as your name, email address, and phone number. I will carefully review your comments and share them with the author and editors who worked on the book.

Email: feedback@quepublishing.com

Mail: Greg Wiegand
            Editor-in-Chief
            Que Publishing
            800 East 96th Street
            Indianapolis, IN 46240 USA

Reader Services

Visit our website and register this book at informit.com/register for convenient access to any updates, downloads, or errata that might be available for this book.

INTRODUCTION

Content-ment.

That's what marketers of all stripes—from tiny, family businesses to multinational conglomerates—are achieving though creating and disseminating content through digital channels: websites, social media networks, blogs, video-sharing sites, newsletters, and more.

Instead of *advertising*, the shift is toward *publishing*. Instead of buying media, you can roll your own and "be there" when potential customers are researching purchase decisions and gather information about products and services.

The challenge? Learn how to think like a publisher to market in digital channels. Content marketing isn't merely a tactic; it's a strategy. Companies that successfully address customer needs and questions with content add value to conversations that take place online. They position themselves not as "buy me!" banners, but as trusted advisors. Content can shape and create a brand voice and identity. Most of all, content makes a company and its products relevant, accessible, and believable.

> "Content marketing is no longer a nice-to-have. It's a must-have."

Content marketing is no longer a nice-to-have. It's a must-have. It's imperative that businesses create content on an ongoing basis. They can't create just any old content, of course. It must be relevant and high quality. It also must be valuable and drive profitable customer interactions. And it must be about customer needs and customer interests, not ad-speak, which is all about the "me."

Marketers are *buying* less and less media. They're *becoming* the media, and the best of them are actually competing with "real" publications for audience, users, and eyeballs. Some marketers are even beating publishers at their own game.

Content marketing isn't new. Companies have been publishing newsletters and producing filmstrips for decades. But a plethora of low-cost tools and ever-lower barriers to entry puts content creation in everyone's grasp at a time when consumers are becoming more cynical about advertising and are better able to tune it out. (TiVO, anyone?)

The purpose of this book is to help anyone who needs to market a business think more like a publisher to take advantage of content marketing. It explains the different types of content marketing. Do you need to amuse and entertain? Inform? Teach? Provide customer service? You'll also learn to assess how and where you need to focus your own efforts.

This book also provides a review of content channels, from websites and social networks to ebooks and webinars, and explains the advantages and disadvantages of each channel. We'll review how to determine content needs, and we'll assign resources to create and disseminate content, while ensuring that it's accessible to the right audiences.

Finally, this book is intended to spark creativity and inspiration with examples of some of the best (and most disastrous!) examples of content marketing in recent years.

This is all in the hopes this book will help you and your business find content-ment.

—Rebecca Lieb
  New York City, 2011

Foreword

I first started using the term content marketing *back in 2001. Until that point, it had rarely been heard or used. Marketing and publishing professionals used a number of terms to describe the concept of brands telling stories to attract and retain customers: custom publishing, custom media, customer media, customer publishing, member media, private media, branded content, corporate media, corporate publishing, corporate journalism, and branded media (just to name a few).*

Of all these, why content marketing?

Let's first start at the beginning.

Marketing, as defined by Merriam-Webster, is the action or business of promoting and selling products or services. Traditionally, companies have done this by buying attention through the use of advertising and promotion through other people's content. For example, if my customers read the leading trade magazine, I would buy an advertisement in that magazine in the hopes that I could divert their attention long enough to make an impact on my sales. It's the same for television, radio, and even buying display advertising on the Web.

In addition to advertising, marketers try to get their *stories* placed in traditional media. The biggest brands in the world still spend billions on trying to get coverage from the press.

This type of marketing is not going away, but considering the thousands of messages that consumers are inundated with on a daily basis, it's harder and harder to cut through the clutter.

Enter content marketing. What if, instead of buying attention, we create content that is so informative, valuable, and compelling that it positively affects the lives of our prospects and customers, and makes an impact on our business? What if, instead of the traditional media, WE became the expert resource for our customers?

What could that do for your business?

Online, in person and in print, how do you position yourself as the expert in your industry and become the true resource? The answer: through great and consistent content.

Everyone creates *content*…but to be *content marketing*, it needs to do something for your business. That's why the term *content marketing* has resonated so much with marketing professionals…it's content that makes an impact, both on your customers and your bottom line.

Content Marketing Is Not New

Content marketing has been used since the dawn of cave paintings. John Deere and its customer magazine *The Furrow* is given credit for the first content marketing initiative. At that time, farmers needed to be educated on the latest in technology so they could be more successful. Instead of buying attention, they created a print content initiative in 1895, teaching farmers all about the latest in technology and trends for farmers. More than 100 years later and with 1.5 million in distribution to 40 countries, *The Furrow* could be the most successful content marketing initiative in history.

Since then, thousands of companies have used content marketing (to an extent), but never have we seen marketing professionals focus so much on content marketing as we do today.

Why?

First, the barriers to entry are gone. As Newt Barrett and I discussed in our first book, *Get Content Get Customers*, the following reasons have left the door wide open for brand marketers to become THE publishers in their industry:

- Buyers accept content from corporate sources more than ever. In other words, you don't have to be *The Wall Street Journal* to find and engage readers.

- Buyers find 99% of purchase information by themselves. The consumer is now in complete control and doesn't care much for your sales processes.

- Shrinking media budgets are leaving an opportunity for YOU. The traditional media model is hurting, and many of those media companies aren't investing in content areas that YOU can cover more effectively.

- The cost of content creation and distribution has significantly decreased. Frankly, with tools like WordPress, the technology is essentially free, and Google, email, and better access to databases let everyone have and use the *tools* of publishing.

- Content expertise is everywhere. Journalists, who in the past thought of corporate content creation as the dark side, are now more than open to working with corporate marketers on their content marketing initiatives.

But perhaps most important, and as Rebecca details specifically in *Content Marketing*, is there another way? Content marketing is not an option anymore. If you want to grow your business, attract new customers, and build long-term relationships with your current customers, you MUST have a content marketing strategy. You have two choices: to inform your customers at the right time with valuable and relevant content, OR entertainment. Good content marketing, as Rebecca discusses, does both.

Although *Get Content Get Customers* showed marketing professionals *the way*, *Content Marketing* will show you how to make this work for your business. Take this book, dog ear it, highlight it, share it with your team, and take the next step to becoming THE informational expert to your customers and prospects.

That's what content marketing can do and will do for your business. Just read on and make it happen. Good luck!

—Joe Pulizzi

Joe Pulizzi is the founder of the Content Marketing Institute and co-author of both *Get Content Get Customers* and *Managing Content Marketing: The Real-World Guide for Creating Passionate Subscribers to Your Brand*. Joe can be reached at joe@junta42.com, or just Google him at "Joe Pulizzi."

1

What Is Content Marketing, Anyway?

"Your customers have chosen the moment—all you have to do is be ready."

Have you ever picked up a company's brochure or flyer? Watched an infomercial or a shopping channel on television? Ordered a product DVD explaining the benefits of a new mattress or a vacation destination? Leafed through a company newsletter? Read the little comic strip in a packet of Bazooka bubble gum?

All these are a few (but by no means an exhaustive list) of the ways companies use content to market their products and services to customers and to prospective buyers.

Content marketing, in other words, is nothing new. Companies having been creating and distributing content for many years, both to attract new business and to retain existing customers. However, here's the point of differentiation from more traditional forms of marketing and advertising: Using content to sell isn't selling, or sales-ey. It isn't advertising. It isn't push marketing, in which messages are sprayed out at groups of consumers. Rather, it's a pull strategy—it's the marketing of attraction. It's being there when consumers need you and seek you out with relevant, educational, helpful, compelling, engaging, and sometimes entertaining information.

When customers and prospects come to *you*, rather than the other way around, the advantages are obvious. They're interested, open, and receptive. Your customers have chosen the moment—all you have to do is be ready. And it spares you much of the headaches and expense of outreach marketing efforts:

- Media planning and buying.

- Direct mail dumps.

- Spraying and praying in an era in which browsers can be configured to block ads, spam filters can be sending your email campaigns into oblivion, digital video recorders are making TV spots optional, and consumers are emptying much of the content of their mailboxes into the Recycling Bin.

There's really no debate over the benefits of tune-in versus tune-out, of pull versus push.

A Roper Public Affairs poll found 80% of business decision makers prefer to get information about a company from articles rather than from ads. Some 70% say content marketing makes them feel closer to the sponsoring company, and 60% believe company content helps them make better product decisions.

Content marketing aids in brand recognition, trust, authority, credibility, loyalty, and authenticity. Content marketing can help accomplish these tasks for a variety of constituencies, and on several levels: for the organization it represents, for a company's products and services, and for the employees who represent the business or service.

Content marketing creates value and helps people. It answers questions and provides foundational information. It makes customers and clients more educated and informed, so they feel they can make purchase decisions, or, in organizations, to recommend purchases to colleagues or superiors. It's used by marketers large and small and by those selling business-to-business (B2B) and business-to-consumer (B2C). Some are using content to augment traditional advertising campaigns. Others are leveraging content to completely replace more traditional forms of advertising and marketing. Content can spark customer engagement at all stages of the buying cycle, including helping to establish an ongoing relationship when a prospect becomes a customer. Content can reinforce an existing relationship, inspire upselling, cross-selling, renewals, upgrades, and referrals.

Digital Changed Everything

Although content marketing is hardly new—after all, businesses have been publishing newsletters and brochures practically since the advent of the printing press—the rise of the Internet and other digital channels, particularly social media, has significantly lowered the bar (and the costs) of leveraging content to profitably attract clients and prospects.

Websites. Blogs. YouTube. eBooks. Downloadable whitepapers. Twitter. Facebook. LinkedIn. Google+. Search engines. All these channels (and many, many more) remove many of the hard cost barriers that were once a mandatory part of creating and disseminating great content. No more paper, printing, shipping, warehousing, postage, filmstock, processing, and developing. Many of the physical and logistical hurdles to creating and disseminating great content are gone.

Although content marketing may be cheaper thanks to digital innovations, it certainly isn't free (even if your Facebook account is), nor has digital made it any easier. Consistently delivering quality content to a target audience requires thought, work, originality, strategy, experimentation, and persistence. A plethora of potential outlets for content online (the options seem to multiply every day) add complexity to the choices you must make about what content to create, in what form, and how to disseminate it—not to mention measuring its effectiveness. One thing is certain: Digital channels overwhelmingly account for the preponderance of content marketing outlets, as Figure 1.1 illustrates.

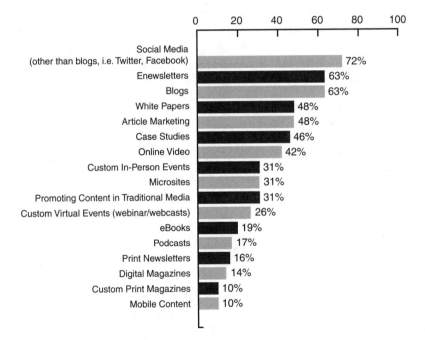

Figure 1.1   *Content Marketing Usage By Tactic.*

Research from this same MarketingProfs/Junta42 study, conducted in 2010, found that 60% of marketers planned to increase content marketing spending in the coming year. Content already accounts for more than 33% of marketing budgets—often double that in smaller organizations. Overwhelmingly, all these efforts and budgets are flowing into digital channels.

> "Be prepared to experiment. Be prepared to fail—but make sure your learn from those failings."

The aim of this book is to help you get a handle on content marketing in digital channels. I examine tactics, strategies, and the myriad channels available to content marketers. I provide case studies from brands both large and small in the hope that they enlighten or inspire.

You should bear in mind that when it comes to content marketing, there really are no rules. There are best practices, to be sure. Aside from common sense notions (such as checking spelling and grammar; if it's a video, it should probably contain moving images and audio), there are no hard and fast rules, only guidelines. The content that works to support *your* business won't be what works for *another* company with a different audience, offering, and personality.

If there's a single thing that deserves to be said before you dive in, it's this: Be prepared to experiment. Be prepared to fail—but make sure your learn from those failings. And above all, have fun. Creating interesting, compelling, original, educational, diverting, immersive, entertaining, and attractive content can be just as valuable and inspiring for the creator as it is for its intended audience.

So have fun! And learn a lot.

2

Why Is Content Important *Now?*

"Content is the bait. It's what captures eyeballs, ears, attention, and engagement."

Content is king.

Anyone who's ever worked in publishing or broadcast media has heard this familiar mantra ad infinitum. In media, content is the bait. It's what captures eyeballs, ears, attention, and engagement. It's part of a time-honored contract with consumers: We'll give you content, you give us attention—but you'll have to agree to get ads or commercials as part of the bargain. The traditional media model is interruptive marketing.

That model still holds true, of course, and will continue to do so. But these days, traditional media is on a continual decline. Newspapers, television, radio, and magazines, although hardly on the verge of extinction, are nevertheless experiencing catastrophic disruption. Circulation and tune-in are sinking. Journalists are losing their jobs in record numbers.

Consider Figure 2.1. According to eMarketer, the time consumers are spending with media is seriously out of whack with the types of media advertisers are buying to reach them.

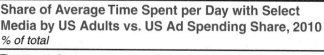

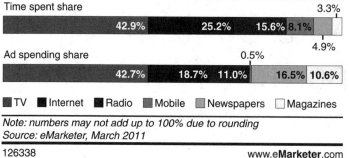

Share of Average Time Spent per Day with Select Media by US Adults vs. US Ad Spending Share, 2010
% of total

	TV	Internet	Radio	Mobile	Newspapers	Magazines
Time spent share	42.9%	25.2%	15.6%	8.1%	3.3%	
Ad spending share	42.7%	18.7%	11.0%	0.5%	16.5%	10.6%

Note: numbers may not add up to 100% due to rounding
Source: eMarketer, March 2011

126338   www.**eMarketer**.com

Figure 2.1 *Share of average time spent per day with select media by U.S. adults versus U.S. ad spending share, 2010.*[1]

Meanwhile, the rise of the Internet and other forms of digital media has created meaningful shifts and changes not only in the way media are consumed, but also in the way various channels are created, found, and disseminated. What powers that fundamental shift is, simply, content and technology platforms that make creating and disseminating content within everyone's grasp.

You may not be able to afford to buy a television network, but nothing's stopping you from creating your own YouTube channel. The cost of launching a newspaper or magazine is prohibitive—and risky. Want to set up a blog? Go for it. A basic blog can be up and running in minutes, and will cost nothing but your time.

Certainly consumers are jumping on these digital trends (see Figure 2.2). Consider the astronomical growth of Facebook, Twitter, YouTube, or other content platforms that didn't exist a decade ago (or in some cases, even five years ago). It took television and even the VCR decades to reach these content platforms' levels of use.

One primary change came with search. Some 90% or more (depending on your sources) of buying decisions begin with a web search. And on the Internet, practically no one's searching for an ad. Depending on where they are in the purchase cycle, they're searching for information, recommendations, research, reviews, authority, and credibility. And when they find the information they seek, they're sharing it with others involved in the purchase decision: A friend, a spouse, a colleague, or their boss, or perhaps they're throwing out that information to a trusted network to vet it or to validate their position in the decision-making process.

1 Source: eMarketer

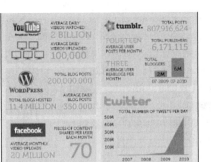

Figure 2.2   *The content boom.*

As Figure 2.3 illustrates, search marketing professionals are working overtime to keep up with this trend. For the first time in 2011, search engine optimization efforts were more directed toward optimizing social media programs than toward more basic activities such as increasing website visibility with links and keywords.

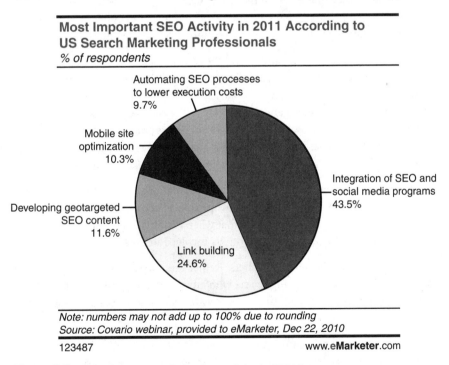

Figure 2.3   *Search engine optimization activity in 2011.*[21]

That's not something you do with an ad, either. Online, ads are hardly searchable, much less shareable.

2 *Source: eMarketer*

Content can also create a virtuous circle in tandem with search engine optimization (SEO) efforts. More content helps a brand, product, service, or company rank higher in search engine results—provided that content is useful, helpful, relevant, or engaging. People talking about that content in social media channels creates links to the content, which in turn further elevates it, search-wise. It's a win-win situation that will be discussed in detail in Chapter 10, "Overview of Content Channels."

Content marketing is also coming to the fore as marketers realize the importance of focusing not only on the buying cycle, but also equally on the sales cycle. Marketers are then flipping the funnel over entirely as they quickly learn that customer service, reputation management, branding, positioning, and public relations (PR) are occurring in digital channels as well as positioning, lead generation, and nurturing.

> "Nine out of ten businesses—across all industries and companies large and small—are incorporating content into the marketing mix."

Businesses of all kinds are adapting, and they're learning how to create great content. A 2010 study conducted by the Business Marketing Association and American Business Media, in conjunction with MarketingProfs and Junta42, surveyed 1,100 marketers in North America and found nine out of ten businesses—across all industries and companies large and small—are incorporating content into the marketing mix. On average, they're spending a quarter of their marketing budgets on content, and over half said they plan to increase that investment in the coming year.

These marketers know content can provide the solutions prospective buyers are seeking when they use search. They know prospects need to be educated before making buying decisions. They know that when credible, trustworthy information is found, it can easily be shared with others involved in the buying process.

They know they can become publishers. Rather than invest time, money, and resources buying or influencing media with advertising or public relations campaigns, savvy marketers can redirect the flow of that money to *become* the media.

Marketers worldwide have caught on to these strategies. Although, as Figure 2.4 illustrates, most still rely on print to distribute at least some of their content, virtually all marketers have made digital the centerpiece of any content distribution strategy.

Case in point: For many years, I was editor-in-chief of the top online publication covering the digital marketing industry. Our bread and butter was selling ads to marketing technology companies and publishing those ads in our email newsletters and on the website.

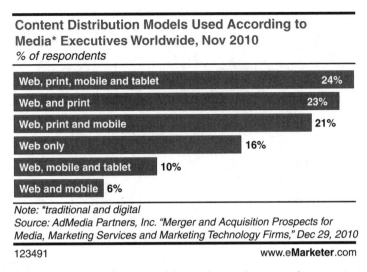

Figure 2.4 *Content distribution modelss used according to media executives worldwide, Nov. 2010.*[3]

HubSpot is a marketing technology company—one that would have been a hot prospect to my former employer's ad sales team. But no longer. A serious, long-term commitment to content marketing means the company features more than 50 digital marketing case studies on its website—all with videos. The site attracts roughly one million unique visitors per month. It sends email newsletters to more than 700,000 subscribers who have opted in to receive them. More than 100,000 people follow the company on Twitter, while another 50,000 track the company's LinkedIn updates. As a result, the company is spending little on other sales and marketing efforts.

And I promise you, these numbers *seriously* compete with the subscriber, following, and website traffic statistics of the major editorial property I led just a few short years ago.

Consumers have come to expect content from brands and the companies they do business with. More and more, marketing is structured to supply content and to enable customers to use it, interact with it, and share it.

To sell, engage, educate, and inform in a highly competitive online environment, the time for marketers to embrace content marketing is now.

3 Source: eMarketer

3

You're a Publisher. Think Like One.

"Rolling your own media brings with it a new set of challenges."

IBM recently published research finding that about 80% of those who begin a corporate blog never post more than five entries. They stop. Give up. Leave it abandoned by the side of what was once called the information super-highway.

And that's just blogging.

The Internet is littered with never-updated websites, near-tweetless Twitter accounts, expressionless Facebook pages, and no-one-home YouTube channels. In the rush to adopt content marketing as a tactic, too many marketers forget that if you're continually publishing, you have to think like...a publisher.

Increasingly, marketing is no longer about buying media (the advertising model). Media is cheap—or often even free. But rolling your own media brings with it a new set of challenges. Chief among those challenges is coming up with enough content to fill all those blank pages, blog posts, profiles, and such, and doing so on a regular basis, not just in a one-off burst of week one enthusiasm.

And hey, this is really nothing new. Coming up with new stuff to say has been an issue for content marketers since the days of the corporate newsletter. Only now, there are even more virtual pages to fill with even more information—and in more multimedia formats.

Who's good at solving that dilemma? Publishers. If you want to win at the content game, it's time you started thinking like one.

In short, brands are media. Marketers are editors, or at least need to start thinking like editors and producers if they don't want to come up shorthanded. So herewith, steps toward publisher-think help marketers get beyond that accusatory blank white page and start thinking like a true content professional.

Here are 14 steps to get you there:

1. **Know your audience**—This couldn't be simpler or more self-evident, but the importance of knowing *who* you're producing content for cannot be overstated. Customers? Prospects? Fans? Industry peers? Colleagues? The media? Some or all of the above? Selecting topics and tailoring messaging is a whole lot easier when you know who's on the receiving end.

2. **Define key themes and messages**—Now that you know who you're addressing, what is it, broadly speaking, you want to communicate to them? Don't just focus on your product, service, or business here, but do some thinking as to how it relates to an audience's real-world concerns. If you're a local business, you may want to weave broader local themes into your content. If you're hawking something with a high consideration curve, education and learning may be part of your messaging. Use your knowledge of your audience, your tone of voice, and the broader informational environment in which you reside to inform themes and messaging.

3. **Establish a frequency framework**—Half the journalists I know (and being one, I know quite a few) say they write for periodicals because they need deadlines to produce something. In the trade, it's called *feeding the beast*. You may not need to blog, or write, or tweet, or status-update every day, but once per month is probably not adequate, and you risk the whole endeavor tipping off the cliff. Create a schedule for content updates, and adhere to it. Map out potential stories, features, or other content in advance so that when the deadline looms, you'll have a sense of what's due. Falling into a rhythm beats falling out of visibility altogether.

4. **Create a detailed editorial calendar**—An editorial calendar plugs directly into the frequency framework. Just as your local newspaper has

a food and dining feature on Wednesdays, an expanded entertainment section on Fridays, and home and gardening every Thursday, mapping a type of content to your frequency framework is a great step forward in terms of making relevant content happen on a reasonably frequent schedule.

5. **Develop regular features and rubrics**—Creating a few regularly appearing content elements is one of the oldest editorial tricks in the book. Comics, horoscopes, weather, and film listings help round off a newspaper's offerings and keep readers coming back for more. Moreover, when you have these regular features, they're all but auto-populating. Highlights of the week, links to other relevant content, or a quote of the day are just a few down-and-dirty ideas to keep the flow of content constantly bubbling.

6. **Interview**—Interviews probably belong in item #5, but they are notable enough to warrant discussion on their own. Are your own ideas drying up? Talk to others, whether they're experts in your field, enthusiastic users, or people in your company. Make a list of potential interview subjects, and consider making interviews a regular content feature.

7. **Go multimedia**—Content isn't limited to text alone, of course. Images, photos, videos, and audio files expand and enhance your content offerings. Blogging? Posts accompanied by a graphic image draw attention to themselves and attract far more clickthroughs than naked-text posts. Don't take my word for it—give it a shot. Your web metrics bear this one out.

8. **Enlist expert contributors, and provide them with guidelines**—You don't have to go it alone. Look around at your coworkers, colleagues, and professional network. There are lots of potential content contributors out there. Often, all you have to do is ask, either for one-off contributions or regular features. You'll want to consider a budget item in this category to incentivize timely and authoritative contributions from really desirable commentators.

9. **Create User-Generated Content**—User-generated content is, of course, a whole new route to ensuring content is created for you, be it comments, ratings and reviews, or contests. With clearly defined guidelines and expectations and a little bit of polite asking, you may be surprised at how much content is created *for* you rather than *by* you.

10. **Opine and editorialize**—A frequent stumbling block to content creation is when the creators think they're obligated to be first to break a piece of news. Unless it's news about you, this is not a winning strategy.

It's a big Internet out there, and news is traveling at the speed of fiber optic cable. News has become commoditized. It's not easy to get the exclusive scoop on a revolution in the Middle East, or who just won the pennant. By the time you've typed it, it's on the web wall-to-wall. Leave breaking news to the pros. Divest yourself of the notion that you're a reporter and instead become an expert observer and interpreter of what news *means* to your audience. Establish yourself, your company, or your brand as a thought leader, not as a deadline reporter.

> "Divest yourself of the notion that you're a reporter and instead become an expert observer and interpreter."

11. **Turn on comments and feedback**—Whatever digital platform you're creating content for, ensure comments and feedback mechanisms are in place, easy to use, and monitored. This not only creates a platform for participation, it's a gauge of how well you're doing, what excites and interests your audience, and will doubtless feed in ideas for shaping and improving future content. Communicate, but don't lecture or preach.

12. **Listen**—Listen to what others in your space are saying, and do so outside the parameters of your own comments section. Set up topic alerts for your relevant themes. Get out there and participate in what others are saying within your arena of expertise. It's the editorial, not to mention the social media equivalent of leaving the house.

13. **Recycle**—Once a piece of content is published, nurture and evolve it. Publishers follow up on news, track trends as they develop, and return to stories to examine long-term effects. They may cover a news item and then editorialize or voice an opinion about the development. They add video or graphics to embellish a point that was made in print. You get the idea: Create more opportunity for the content that you have to get out there.

14. **Capture**—In a number of respects, publishing has always been a form of lead-generation. Consumer publishers use subscriber, viewership and newsstand information, and data to profile customers, and they market those numbers and demographics to their advertisers. Business-to-business (B2B) publishers capture leads for that purpose, and often also to market ancillary products and services to that audience, be it research reports, conferences, or other special offers.

4

What Kind of Content Are You?

"The first rule of knowing what kind of content you'll create is knowing who you're creating it for."

The title of this chapter is something of a trick question. Sure, content marketing means developing content around your business, your products, and your services. But that content isn't supposed to exist in some you-oriented void. Content is aimed externally: at customers, prospects, buyers, brand advocates, bloggers, the media, people participating in social networks, and potentially employees (if you're recruiting).

So the first rule of knowing what kind of content you'll create is knowing who you're creating it for. This will not only help you determine what kind of content, but also in what form and where content will appear. Blogs? YouTube videos? Tweets?

You'll never know until you begin creating personas.

Personas?

Personas are used in digital marketing for many purposes, not just content market-ing. They're woven into website design, usability, navigation, advertising, and mar-keting messages. They're used in offline scenarios, too, particularly in the retail sector. The idea behind personas is that you can't connect with your customers (and other constituencies) if you don't know who they are. Obviously, you can't know each person individually, but do a little research, and different audience seg-ments start falling into pretty well-defined characters with distinct characteristics.

Although books have been written about the art and science of developing user personas, the idea is to boil your audience down to a handful of distinct individu-als, each representing a group you're serving—or trying to reach. Personas have names, faces, and real personalities.

Following are three example personas:

- Jill is 28, and a highly competitive person, both at work and in her per-sonal life. Social status is important to her, and she appreciates these qualities in others. She tends to make impulsive decisions and is quick to turn to the Internet to accomplish tasks so long as she is able to get what she needs quickly and efficiently. She seeks verifiable results and quantifiable bottom lines. Social interaction in the process of a business transaction is not important to her. She'll willingly pay more to get extra benefits or features. Jill is unmarried and does not see marriage in her near future.

- James, 36, is Internet savvy and is online in excess of 10 hours per day. He has multiple email accounts and does all his shopping and banking online, often from his iPad or iPhone. James works for an ecommerce company and has just purchased a modest one-bedroom condo in the suburbs outside a large metropolitan city.

- Stacy, 34, is a soccer mom and the main shopper for her family, living in a semi-rural community. Outside of using email to communicate with friends and family, she's intimidated by technology and inexperi-enced with the Internet. She is well educated and usually confident, but she doesn't really trust online shopping sites that require credit card information, and she's leery of joining social networks. She's heard too much bad news about identity theft and privacy and thinks it's safer just to avoid these potentially risky areas.

Your content won't connect with customers (or prospects) if you don't know who they are, and it's unlikely they're some amorphous mono-person. They're disparate individuals who likely fall into half a dozen or so distinct categories. People in each of these categories search differently. They discuss different things on different social networks. How they decide what to buy, or what to recommend to their friends, family, or colleagues at work, is different and distinct. They have different predilections and different preferences. Instead of creating content for everyone, you're talking to Stacy, or Jill, or James.

So how do you go about creating personas? Start by digging into data. Look at website analytics. Where are people coming from? What keywords and phrases do they use to find you (and your competitors)? How does your conversion data pan out from those metrics?

> "Your content won't connect with customers (or prospects) if you don't know who they are."

You can use a variety of tools to collect and parse this data, as well as social media listening tools, services that break out a site's demographic information, and services such as Flowtown and Rapleaf that tease social network data out of your email lists (assuming you have them). Then there's that tried-and-true method: the customer survey. (Offering the chance to win a $50 Amazon gift certificate is a great way to encourage participation.)

After you've collected all this data, analyzed it, and segmented it into personas, it's important to regularly revisit persona profiles. After all, they're not etched in stone.

When personas have been developed, you'll know who you're talking to and writing for. You may even get a clearer idea as to whether pink or cerulean blue should be the dominant color on a web page or in a photo or video. You'll have a clearer understanding of where your personas congregate online and how you might approach them.

Think of it this way: If you were trying to get a pretty girl to go out with you, you'd likely adapt a radically different approach when coming on to the bookish graduate student in the library, as opposed to the flamboyant party girl in the red spangled dress at a disco.

Well, *wouldn't* you?

Every business has its own set of unique personas. Some have only three or four, whereas others have a dozen or more. Although all your content marketing initiatives ought to be addressed directly to one of your identified personas (although it's perfectly possible that one content initiative may cover two or more profiles), all content marketing tends to fall into a specific set of categories.

Let's consider them. The next few chapters break down the different content categories.

5

Content That Entertains

People don't remember facts, figures, numbers, or statistics. But they recall, and spread, stories.

Once upon a time...

Tell me a story...

There's nothing more central to the human experience than storytelling. Being immersed in a narrative that makes you laugh or cry passes the time, is fun, and makes you want to go out and share the tale, the experience, the pathos, or the humor. People don't remember facts, figures, numbers, or statistics. But they recall, and spread, stories.

And what's entertainment—be it a story, a game, a movie, or an episode of a recurring drama—if not content?

As digital marketing became mainstream, so did marketing campaigns that engaged, intrigued, and entertained Internet users. One landmark example was Burger King's Subservient Chicken. Without mentioning Burger King at all, the quirky, bizarre, and not a little perverse website featured someone wearing a giant chicken suit that obeyed (almost) any command a user typed into a text box (see Figure 5.1) with the tag line "Chicken the way you like it."

The campaign went mega-viral. Millions of consumers spent thousands of hours telling the chicken what to do. Sales of Burger King's TenderCrisp sandwich spiked during the campaign.

Figure 5.1   The Subservient Chicken cuts a rug after being ordered to dance. www.bk.com/en/us/campaigns/subservient-chicken.html

Another highly successful early example of entertainment content was American Express' heralded Seinfeld/Superman campaign. The online component derived from a series of commercials starring Jerry Seinfeld and his friend, the animated Superman, and were directed by Barry Levinson (see Figure 5.2). Online, the campaign expanded. Not only could the amusing commercials be viewed in their entirety, but users could watch behind-the-scenes production footage, tour Jerry's apartment, send e-cards, play a sing-along game, and have other interactive adventures that take advantage of the digital medium. The campaign grabbed headlines and talk show appearances by its stars, sparking buzz and conversation—and it lives on nearly a decade later on the dedicated website, as well as on YouTube.

Figure 5.2   Superman relates a story to Jerry Seinfeld in the American Express campaign.

So successful was Jerry Seinfeld as a shill for American Express that a couple of years later Microsoft hired him to appear in another series of humorous web-only videos, co-starring with Microsoft founder Bill Gates (see Figure 5.3). Like the American Express spots, as well as Burger King's, the sell was a soft one. In this case, Microsoft wasn't even mentioned, merely represented by Gates' presence. Although the spots were web-only, the publicity value of the duo was enough to warrant plenty of pickup in mainstream print and broadcast media.

Figure 5.3   Hanging with another famous friend: This time, Jerry's listening to Bill Gates.

And no, you don't have to be a star to create successful, engaging, creative marketing content. You don't even have to have the budget to hire one. Case in point: Blendtec.

Tom Dickson, the high-end blender manufacturer's CEO, bought a white lab coat, a pair of goggles, and a URL: www.willitblend.com. Total investment: $1,000. Dickson noticed that every time he jammed a 2 × 2 board into a blender to test it, people in the plant would stop what they were doing to watch. He figured this might translate to the web. Over the years, and always under the motto, "Don't try this at home," Dickson has blended iPhones, iPads, a crowbar, glow sticks, cameras, running shoes, a can of pork and beans, a video camera…you get the idea (see Figure 5.4).

"You don't have to be a star to create successful, engaging, creative marketing content. You don't even have to have the budget to hire one."

Figure 5.4   Don't try this at home, kids! Tom Dickson "blends" a running shoe.

Sales of Dickson's blenders rose more than 700%.

Will It Blend has been on every list of the top viral videos every week for years. The campaign has spawned literally hundreds of millions of views and is so popular that Blendtec is actually *selling its marketing.* Viewers find what's essentially an advertisement for Blendtec—Dickson doing product demonstrations—so entertaining that they're willing to shell out $10 to buy a DVD compilation of the episodes. In other words, the campaign, which regularly rolls out new episodes of Dickson pulverizing stuff in Blendtec blenders, is also keeping the brand top-of-mind for consumers who may not be in the market for a blender today, but who will certainly be thinking of his products the next time they're ready to buy a blender. They've become fans, and the product isn't only demonstrably effective, it also has a personality.

It bears mentioning that Blendtec's content marketing doesn't begin and end with its YouTube channels and WillItBlend.com. That site links to Blendtec.com (and vice versa, of course), where visitors can find not only blenders, but also demonstration videos, recipes, installation tips, and more.

Online video is clearly one of the best channels for content that entertains and engages and that gets passed along. There are dozens more examples of viral (and business) success:

- IBM has a YouTube channel dedicated to entertaining and funny videos around (of all things) mainframe computers entitled *Mainframe—The Art of the Sale.*
- Dove's Pro Aging campaign was a runaway success.
- The Old Spice Guy rocketed actor Isaiah Mustafa to fame.
- Ikea produced a popular series around the concept "Easy to Assemble." It also created an amazing video of what happens when you release dozens of cats in a UK store.

- Not long ago, Air New Zealand put an in-flight safety video starring exercise guru Richard Simmons online. Within hours, it was the most-tweeted video in the world, and it had racked up more than a million views.

Video isn't the only way to entertain, of course. Take Woot, the online deal-a-day retailer that rose to prominence—and an acquisition by Amazon—through its ingenious use of content to tell stories around rather mundane products. On any other website, a recent T-shirt offered for sale might have been described as "Black & white print design on a navy shirt. Sizes: S, M, L, XL."

Here's how Woot describes this perfectly mundane product.

WE'RE GONNA GO THE DISTANCE, MANDI. WE'RE GONNA MAKE IT.

It's the Senior Spring Formal, babe. We've been through a lot of crazy stuff, you know? Like that time my buddy Jason ate 10 Double Decker Tacos at the Taco Bell. Or that time I accidentally spilled root beer in your mom's Civic. Wow. It seems like just yesterday we were nervous about our locker assignments as Freshmen, but that was three whole years ago.

So here's what I wanted to say, baby. I love you. I want to be with you. And I know that no matter where life takes us, even though we know you're going to go to NYU or something and become a fashion designer or the next Lady Gaga and I'm going to win a national championship at a big state school before playing shortstop for either the Giants or the Cubs depending on who offers me more money, we're going to be together forever. That's why even though we're only 17 I'm pledging my eternal love and devotion. *Forever.*

And that's why I think we should do it.

What? Where are you going? Come on! Oh my god the guys totally said you'd react this way. What?! Only Ryan and Jason and Tim and Suraj and the other Ryan and Scott. Oh like *you* don't talk about *me* with *your* friends. You are so selfish! I swear, we've been going out for like three *WEEKS* and I don't have *one* braggable sexual conquest yet! This is ridiculous!

Yeah? Well I hate you anyway! You're so stupid! And everyone thinks I can do better than you anyway, I don't know why I even stuck around! Yeah, we'll see what your best friend Jill thinks! I'M TEXTING HER RIGHT NOW YOU STUPID JERK! I want my jacket back *AND* my Green Day CD. I was a fool to think you'd ever truly understand those lyrics on the level I do. Whatever! I HOPE YOU HAVE THE WORST SENIOR YEAR EVER! I HOPE YOU DIE!

Awwwww, baby. See what you do to me? See how much I *love* you?

Wear this shirt: If you're on a mission to complete the "My wardrobe is entirely by patrickspens" set.

Don't wear this shirt: If you're seriously planning on marrying your high school sweetheart.

This shirt tells the world: "Slow down, Sparky. Some of us have better plans."

We call this color: We'll get married as soon as I get my first shore leave from the Navy.

Design Placement: Centered

Design Size:

3X – S: 11.00" × 18.99"

WXL – WS: 8.25" × 14.24"

K12 – K4: 7.09" × 12.25"

Pantone Colors: White – 284C

Please check our sizing chart before you order. The Woot Tee follows a classic closer-fitting style. If you prefer a baggier look, order a larger size. If there is not a larger size, consider starting a belly-hanging-out trend.

This kind of out-there copy isn't a new idea. You might recall the old print J. Peterman catalogue, now online as well, in which every garment was described by a story. A plain cotton nightshirt on the site is named after Marie Antoinette; the copy that describes it is less a tale of a plain white cotton nightshirt, and more a fable of the life of a queen ruling over the court of Versailles.

Enticing people to buy into a story instead of just a T-shirt or nightshirt works. It gives them a reason to spend time with your brand and products. It gives the brands' and the products' personalities, identities, and stories. It makes people dream—even eagerly anticipate—your next catalog or ecommerce offering.

Don't believe me? Believe the hundreds of thousands of customers who may not have tuned in to Comcast's commercials but who are now eagerly awaiting delivery of their fictitious product, the hottest new pet out there: "petite lap giraffes," as shown in Figure 5.5.

Figure 5.5   But do they shed? A petite lap giraffe relaxes on the sofa.

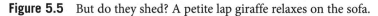

Those old, turn-of-the-century Sears catalogues have long been referred to as the "dream books" or "wish books" of an earlier America. Consumption patterns may have evolved, but basic human nature—the desire to become immersed in compelling, funny, fantastic, or exciting stories—is as strong as ever.

6

Content That Informs and Educates

Information is power, and the Internet is where consumers turn for information. Providing valuable, credible information can be the foundation of a sound business model—something the earliest online businesses learned in a hurry.

Take Autobytel, for example. Autobytel, which was launched in 1995, was the web's first car-buying website that supplied consumers with information they'd never had access to before—how much automotive dealers paid for new cars. "The dealers hated it," recalls Thomas Heshion, a former executive.

Sure, Autobytel will always be remembered as the first dot-com to advertise during the Super Bowl, but it's thriving more than a decade later because it supplies information that helps car buyers better understand what they're buying and how much they should pay for it. In short, the information Autobytel provides informs and educates.

Some marketers sell products that are dead simple. Everyone intuitively gets what they do. Some examples:

> "Rather than just selling, companies are sharing: knowledge, expertise, and how-to."

- Combs

- Forks

- Pencils

You know what they are. You know how to use them, and you know why you need them. No further information or explanations are required.

Then, there's the enormous amount of stuff that's just plain more complicated. Some examples:

- HVAC systems

- High-end stereo equipment

- Enterprise software

- Vintage maps

- Real estate

None of these is an off-the-shelf purchase.

The purchase cycle may be long. The considerations around the value proposition and product offerings are dizzying and complex. Sure, you can create awareness with an ad, but often you have to go further. Much further. Potential consumers must be informed and educated about the products and services. The intimidation factor must be removed. Often, particularly in B2B environments, buying decisions are a collaborative process involving groups of people and often multiple business units.

The solution? A content marketing strategy focused on information and education. The following examples show how a variety of companies—from mom 'n' pops to multinational corporate giants—are leveraging educational and informative digital content to help consumers navigate their products and buying processes. Rather than just selling, companies are sharing: knowledge, expertise, and how-to. They know customers who might not have 30 seconds to spend on watching one of their ads might gladly surrender 30 minutes to dive into truly useful content.

Example: Wine Library

Gary Vaynerchuk got roped into joining his family business, Shopper's Discount Liquors, in New Jersey. It didn't take him long to realize that many people enthusiastically collected rare vintages. He rebranded the store as Wine Library and launched a fantastically successful ecommerce site in the late '90s, increasing revenues from $4 million to over $60 million annually. But he didn't stop there.

Wine is a complex and to many, intimidating product category. To increase awareness and sales, Gary took it upon himself to educate customers and potential customers. He launched Wine Library TV, a daily video blog that now attracts some 90,000 daily viewers. Gary's approach to his rarified and somewhat stuffy subject matter is casual and informal—often bordering on irreverent. One of the over 8,000 episodes, for example, is entitled "What Wine Pairs with Cereal?," featuring tastings of vintage wines with entrees such as Cap'n Crunch (see Figure 6.1).

Figure 6.1   *Note the separate pairings for Lucky Charms, Cap'n Crunch, and Cinnamon Toast Crunch in the tongue-in-cheek episode of Wine Library TV.*

As his fame grew—in no small part thanks to leveraging the show's content on Facebook and Twitter—Gary has been able to entice celebrities to participate in Wine Library TV. He now has a radio show on Sirius and is a bestselling author.

Example: Corning

Corning produced a corporate video for shareholders extolling the near-future of high-tech consumer products made of glass. Entitled "A Day Made of Glass," the six-minute video (that's a very long running time on the Internet!) was shown in early 2011 at an investor event (see Figure 6.2). Less than six weeks later, it was the most-watched corporate video of all time, with 8 million YouTube views and climbing (and a great example of recycling content assets, discussed further in Chapter 23, "Listening and Responding").

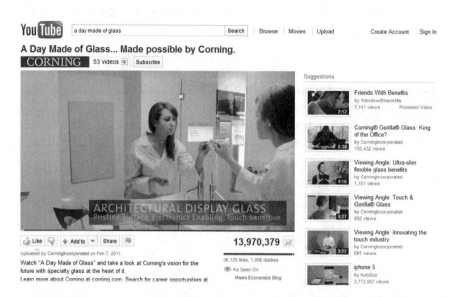

Figure 6.2 *In the not-too-distant future, you'll be checking news and weather on the bathroom mirror, according to Corning's vision of how glass will be combined with technology.*

"It breaks all the rules when you think about it," a spokesman from Corning's agency, Doremus, told the media. "It's six minutes long; it's not funny, it doesn't have celebrities in it, it's not intended to be sent around to your friends." But it is a simple and well-told story, filled with imagination and engaging performances.

Example: Sports Bras

Educational content can also be powerful when it harnesses the authority of an impartial expert. Social media PR expert Sally Falkow was charged with building awareness for HerRoom.com, a women's intimate apparel site. Obviously, in an ecommerce situation, potential customers can't try on the merchandise.

To facilitate sports bra buying decisions, Falkow engaged the services of Dr. Joanna Scurr of Portsmouth University in the UK. Scurr has conducted research into the dynamics of breast movement and what sports bras work best. The campaign consisted of a highly search engine optimized (SEO) press release on Scurr's "bounce test," as well as a podcast in which Scurr discusses her research and findings. On HerRoom.com, shown in Figure 6.3, each sports bra product show is actually a video still. When activated, shoppers can see the actual amount of bounce as models jog in each individual bra.

Figure 6.3   *Videos and a podcast on the dynamics of breast movement during exercise, delivered by an expert, help women make informed decisions about buying the right sports bra.*

Example: Hubspot

Sports bras do pretty much one thing. What if you're a technology company selling a suite of highly complex products that do multiple things? HubSpot is one such company. It offers a software package that encompasses content and social media management, inbound lead analysis, email marketing, website management, and a host of analytics products. Essentially, the company has created a new product category, so even selling to marketers who fundamentally understand most of these principles is complex.

Because much of what the company does centers around content marketing, HubSpot practices what it preaches. The company website is a goldmine of information for marketers, featuring original research, videos, a podcast, webinars, white papers, eBooks, marketing charts and graphs, free online tools, and of course, a blog.

The company also runs communities centered around inbound marketing on Facebook and LinkedIn, as well as an inbound marketing university.

HubSpot is a content marketing powerhouse, churning out as much, or possibly even more content around its inbound marketing offering than a dedicated trade publication would. Of course, that content comes at a price—which isn't monetary.

To take advantage of the most robust content offerings on the site, which are downloads, the exchange is information. The downloader supplies an email address, name, title, and some information about their business. Yes, if you download some of its content, you can expect to hear from a HubSpot rep.

Is it working? In March 2011, three highly respected companies—Salesforce, Google, and Sequoia—endowed HubSpot with an additional $32 million financing round. That's not only an endorsement of what the company is selling, but also how it's selling it. HubSpot is a company that's firmly establishing itself as an authority in its specific niche.

Example: Online Communities

"Online communities are a tried-and-true method of involving customers in products, product decisions, and troubleshooting, creating loyalty and often adding a viral, word-of-mouth dimension."

Condé Nast's Epicurious is one of the oldest and best recipe sites on the web. A feature that attracts readers—and repeat visitors—is the community aspect of the site. Readers comment on recipes and add tweaks or substitutions. It builds loyalty, creates significant amounts of content, and enhances the overall value of the site.

Online communities are a tried-and-true method of involving customers in products, product decisions, and troubleshooting, creating loyalty and often adding a viral, word-of-mouth dimension to informative content. These can, of course, be created by customers with no intervention from a company, but many companies have elected to invest in the benefits communities create.

Communities can amplify customer feedback, helping sponsoring companies to better understand their needs and even guide product development. And the customer focus that communities foster reinforces marketing messages by demonstrating an atmosphere of trust, transparency, and openness.

Tech companies have long been at the forefront of informative, educational community efforts. That's not surprising given they sell complex products to relatively tech-savvy audiences. Apple Discussions is one of the oldest, containing literally thousands of articles, tips, and queries of literally every model of computer, server, iPad, iPhone, monitor, hardware, and software model the company has ever sold.

Online communities can save companies a tremendous amount of time, money, and energy that they would otherwise funnel into customer support. Pauline Ores, the former head of social media at IBM, created a community customer support and feedback forum and was then tasked with training engineers to work in this new channel. Initially, they were reluctant. Yet they quickly saw their workload drop considerably. "They're answering each others' questions!" was one delighted discovery from a staffer tasked with repeatedly having to respond to customer queries via email. Often, it was the same queries, over and over again.

SAP is another company that's developed a successful, robust community. Not only does it inform the network of developers using the company's software products, it contains educational and informative content of its own, such as videos and articles that help users get the most out of community participation and membership.

Microsoft's Xbox community is aimed at a number of different target audiences, all within the purview of console gamers. It offers forums for lovers of music games and family games, as well as incentives: chances to earn points that can be exchanged for games, game add-ons, or even renting movies. Of course, it also helps connect users who want to play games with one another.

American Express created a community in 2007 in which members can help one another, while helping the world. The company is, of course, a major corporate donor. The Members Project opens up that process (the transparency part) and gives cardholders a say in who gets some $4.2 million in charitable donations from the company.

After registering on the site, participants can vote once a week for a charity they think deserves financial support. Every three months, five charities are chosen to receive $200,000 apiece in funding from American Express. Voters are encouraged to use a broad variety of channels to contact friends to help vote up their choices, spreading knowledge of the issues, the needs, and the brand's participation in the process. The site also provides opportunities to volunteer and donate either time or credit card loyalty points to worthy causes.

Branded Content That Informs and Educates

Although American Express's members project certainly is worthy, American Express is better known for leveraging branded content online in support of its marketing efforts.

Branded content is content produced by—or sponsored by—one entity rather than a plethora of advertisers. It's hardly a new concept. How do you think the soap opera got its name? Dating back to early radio and television, companies were wrapping entertainment in exclusive sponsorship. The difference in content marketing is now they're creating all the content, too.

And they're learning that if it's quality informative content (or entertaining content, as shown in Chapter 5, "Content That Entertains," visitors will come. And come back. Because you don't always have to buy media. You can create it.

Its OPEN Forum is described as "a wealth of resources for business owners— videos, articles, blogs, podcasts, and expert advice to boost your business." Aimed at small business owners, the site (see Figure 6.4) resembles an online magazine more than it does a marketing initiative with tips on entrepreneurship, marketing, technology, and money. The only difference? All the ads are for American Express products. Nonetheless, the site is certainly *run* like a magazine, with a team of editors and a stable of high-profile contributors, such as well-known web entrepreneurs Guy Kawasaki and John Battelle. (Battelle, not incidentally, founded Federated Media, the content marketing agency that runs OPEN Forum.)

Figure 6.4   *The American Express site for small business owners looks and feels like a "real" publishing site—and attracts more traffic than many "real" publishing sites do.*

American Express considers OPEN Forum successful enough to have launched what's essentially a spin-off site. Currency has the same high content standards but targets a Gen Y audience with lessons, advice, and how-tos on money management: retirement planning, budgeting, savings, and the like. Both these content sites from American Express feature everything you'd expect in a high-quality publisher site: RSS feeds, social media links, an iPhone app, and newsletter subscriptions.

✉ *Note*

> MasterCard Small Business is a similar initiative from one of the direct
> competitors of American Express.

No wonder media companies are having such a tough time of it.

The most fundamental consumer products have been creating similar online branded content initiatives for years now. At first glance, Baby.com appears to be a site about pregnancy and caring for babies. Which, of course, it is. It's also part of BabyCenter, shown in Figure 6.5, a family of sites devoted to parent and childcare issues launched in 1997. It features a community and a whole host of international sites on the same topics that span the globe from Korea to India to Mexico and Russia—22 in all. The only thing that differentiates Baby.com from any of the other well-designed, richly populated, frequently updated sites on the subject is again that the publisher is also the owner and sponsor; in this case, it's Johnson & Johnson.

Think babies are a niche market? Indeed, they are, but the niche can narrow in branded content. Kimberly-Clark makes Huggies diapers and runs a baby and parenting site that reaches into most of the same areas of content as Baby.com. The Huggies.com brand website features content on every conceivable topic from pregnancy countdowns to feeding and (of course) diapering a new baby and keeping the tyke healthy, entertained, and stimulated through to toddlerhood. Many of the articles and features focus on diapers and keeping the baby clean with wipes, but even more don't. The goal is brand impressions, brand engagement, and becoming a trusted source of information for new mothers.

Figure 6.5 *Note Baby.com's email newsletter sign-up box. It allows Johnson & Johnson to deliver messages that are targeted exactly to an expectant mother's pregnancy phase.*

Branded content can go a lot broader than mothers, babies, Gen Y, and small business owners. Global conglomerates offering a plethora of complex products and services to highly diverse target audiences are turning to content for many of the same reasons consumer package goods manufacturers are: engagement, education, inspiration, trust, and transparency.

Let's return to IBM. The company distilled its product and services offerings down to a single concept: A Smarter Planet. Launched as a symposium in Barcelona in which 600 organizations participated (let's not forget live events are a form of content marketing, too), A Smarter Planet is now a robust editorial website, as you can see in Figure 6.6, dedicated to delivering content on a broad mandate of a topic: "*How we use data. How industries collaborate. How we make a smarter planet.*"

Figure 6.6 *IBM's Smarter Planet takes care to segment its audience into varying groups of potential customers and clients.*

Doesn't sound very bite-sized, does it? IBM is perfectly well aware of that. That's why all the content on the site is organized into carefully designated industry vertical buckets, such as cloud computing, water, food, transportation systems, healthcare, and so on—all segments the company serves. Content offerings are a robust mix of articles, research, video, statistics, and opportunities to attend live events. Much—but not all—of the site content is bylined by top executives at the company, which helps put faces on what is, after all, a rather monolithic entity.

GE's Ecomagination is a similar content marketing initiative. It not only promotes the company's own green initiatives in light rail, wind farms, and the like but also leverages community much in the vein of the American Express Members Project in which participants can submit, discuss, and vote for the best ideas in green, sustainable projects (see Figure 6.7).

Examples of companies that provide digital information to their customers and prospects are nearly endless. Google publishes some 110 blogs, each corresponding to a different product or business unit. Almost all are updated several times per week. Even the U.S. Postal Service (USPS), that stalwart of paper-based marketing, has put its magazine for direct-mail marketers, "Deliver," online.

Figure 6.7   *GE's Ecomagination encourages user participation and has an open, breezy, fresh-air look and feel to the site that keeps it in line with its mission.*

DeliverMagazine.com contains feature stories and columns, polls, video case studies, podcasts, digital versions of the printed magazine, and a series of marketing campaigns whose content focuses on issues of concern to the direct marketing community.

According to a USPS spokesperson, there have been more than 70,000 downloads from the website, as shown in Figure 6.8.

Figure 6.8   *Even that bastion of direct mail marketing, the USPS, recognizes the need to reach marketers, its target audience, with digital information to educate, inform, and persuade them to use the USPS.*

7

Providing Utility

When most people think content, they think written, visual, or audio-visual media: words, pictures, photos, video, audio, and perhaps graphs, charts, and infographics. It can be persuasively argued that in a digital environment, tools count as content, too. They can be educational, informative, helpful, decision and buying aids, entertaining, interactive...and above all, useful.

Think of them as utility content. And think how many times you've used them.

Think financial services sites offering loan calculators, or retirement calculators and applications that do comparative math for different types of mortgages or help calculate a savings goal. Consider how many times you've visited eBay, UPS, USPS.com, or Amazon.com to figure out shipping rates, shipping speed, package tracking, or parcel arrival.

Financial tools extend to automotive dealer sites as well, but so do utilities that help you select and configure a vehicle (see Figure 7.1). Two doors or four? How does red look versus green? How much extra for the souped-up audio system or heated seats? These utilities don't just help prospective buyers make decisions; they also put them into the position of weighing all their options. And it's not only manufacturers who use utilities. Sites such as AutoTraders also have this type of tool, so a buyer can pinpoint the vehicle for sale in her area that comes closest to her dream machine.

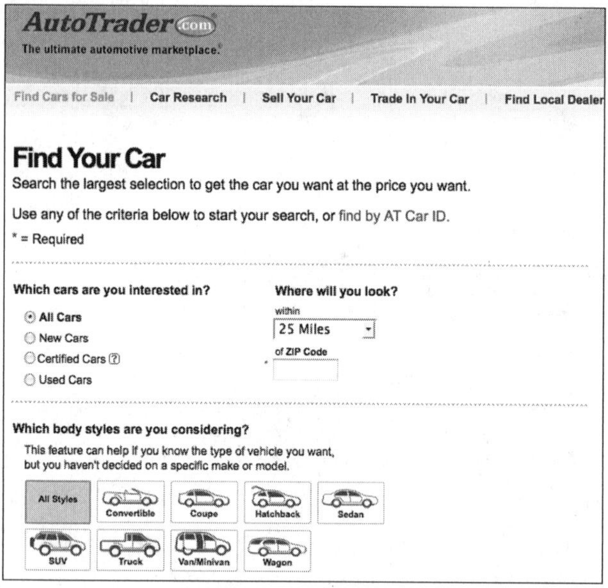

Figure 7.1 *What are the features of your perfect car, and how far would you be willing to travel to get it? AutoTrader has a tool to help you figure out just that.*

These types of utility content not only aid in decision-making, but also help to bring prospects closer to purchase.

Such tools go beyond packages and cars, even getting very personal indeed. Retailers have built tools to help find jeans that will flatter your body type and show you an image of what *you'd* look like in them, not some six-foot tall, 98-pound model. Not dissimilarly, any number of sites allows you to upload a headshot to try a virtual makeover on for size (see Figure 7.2). Testing how different hairstyles and colors or makeup looks online is another step toward conversion, just as it is at the department store counter. It's also a step toward the potential customer, offering them tools and information to help them in buying and decision making.

Utility content can range from the super-simple to the mega-slick. At the low end, it can be as simple as publishing glossaries or dictionaries of highly technical or industry-related terms to help newcomers navigate a new field of knowledge.

Utility can also be a matter of packaging content so that it's easy to consume or use on the go. Obvious examples are publisher sites such as *The New York Times* or *The Wall Street Journal* that are good to go as apps on a smartphone or tablet computer. That same utility shows up when conference or seminar organizers publish agendas in mobile formats that contain functionality such as schedules (official and personalized), directories of who's attending, and perhaps even the event newsletter or a map of the trade show or convention center. Some would argue these are tools, not content. But is there really a reason why content can't be both?

Figure 7.2   *Would you really look better as a blonde? Try it on for size before reaching for the peroxide.*

Many content utilities are, in essence, searchable databases. They're rife in the food industry. No celebrity chef worth his salt is without one. Martha Stewart, Jamie Oliver, and a host of others have searchable recipe databases with additional functionality, such as nutrition information and the ability to churn out a shopping list (see Figure 7.3). Kraft Foods has its own recipe database, complete with apps and additional tools, such as ones that help shoppers find in-season produce. In the same vein, so does Weber's, only its offering is geared toward customers who are interesting in grilling, marinating, and finding food and recipes in line with the company's line of grills and outdoor cooking products.

Fast food outlets from Dairy Queen to Taco Bell to Panera Bread have nutrition calculators for their menu offerings. So do sites for diabetics, and other health- and disease-oriented businesses. Dominos and Pizza Hut offer apps and tools that help you sift through their menus and then order food online or via your phone. Some of these have tracking functionality so that buyers know when their order has been received, is in the oven, and is out for delivery.

> "Even some of the most unlikely products you can think of have come up with ways to provide users with utilitarian content while keeping the brand top-of-mind."

Even some of the most unlikely products you can think of have come up with ways to provide users with utilitarian content while keeping the brand top-of-mind. SitOrSquat, an app sponsored by Charmin toilet tissue, is a geo-location-sensitive database of the best places in the world to find clean restroom facilities (see Figure 7.4). Users have the ability to update the information.

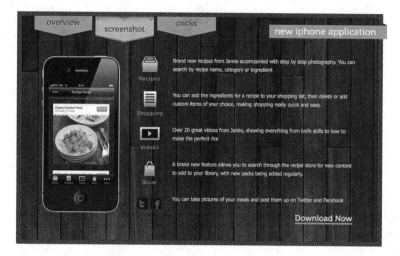

Figure 7.3   *What to cook? What ingredients do you need to cook it? How the heck do you cook it? Jamie Oliver's app shows, and tells.*

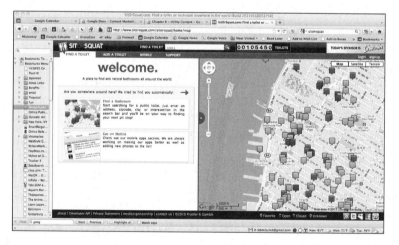

Figure 7.4   *When you gotta go, SitorSquat helps you decide where to go by locating the nearest, cleanest toilet.*

Most major banks offer similar tools that help you find the nearest branch or ATM machine (see Figure 7.5). Chase even allows you to make a deposit online or by smart-phone by taking a digital photo of the check and then uploading it to your account.

Figure 7.5   *Check your balance, even deposit a check—all with your mobile phone.*

There are other ways to help users buy on a geographic basis. Burpee, the venerable seed catalogue, has information on the proper plants and flowers for different growing zones (see Figure 7.6). By entering your zip code on the site, not only is shipping information more accurate, but products are featured that are tailored to your area, as are suggestions for planning and planting a garden. Plan-a-Garden from Better Homes and Gardens has similar functionality: delivering more relevant content to its readers.

Figure 7.6   *How doth your garden grow? Depends on where you live. Burpee's got a tool for that.*

Interactive online tools are almost de rigueur in digital publishing—and remember, brands are now publishers. When I led one of the largest sites covering digital advertising, we published literally hundreds of articles every week. But week in, week out, one of the most-visited pages on the site was the years-old CPM calculator that helped online advertisers calculate how much they were paying for their online advertising. The Laredo Group, a company that offers training in online

> "Interactive online tools are almost de rigueur in digital publishing—and remember, brands are now publishers."

advertising, offers the ROAS calculator, which is a tool that tracks return on advertising spend. Similarly, sites such as DPReview.com allow shoppers to make side-by-side comparisons of different models of digital cameras by price and feature.

Technology companies are, unsurprisingly, big on tools, either to help prospective customers better understand their businesses or to let them sample the more robust commercial versions of their offerings. Both Alexa and Compete offer website ranking and competitive analysis. You can learn a lot, both about how your own site is performing and the power of analytics, by diving into the free versions of their software online.

Search engine marketers often turn to free keyword research tools offered not only by the major search engines, but also by companies such as Wordtracker. Not dissimilar are utilities that analyze on-page keyword density, or tools for email marketers that calculate the likelihood of a message being flagged as spam based on trigger words in the subject line and message body.

Another industry in which content utility is rife is health care. Users can remain engaged and educated when offered the opportunity to calculate their own body mass index, risk of contracting certain types of cancer, or tracking their level and optimum times for fertility.

Big brands bring big splashiness to utility content. Take Nike. Not only does the company offer a sophisticated Shoe Finder to help runners find the right shoe for their style of running, but Nike iD also allows them to custom-design shoes, selecting their own colors and custom sole (see Figure 7.7). Nike has taken utility to the extreme with Nike+, which combines a running shoe and an Apple device that tracks joggers' runs and then logs them online. In this case, customers buy the product not only because of the gold-standard brands (Nike and Apple), but also because the functionality allows them, in effect, to create their own content. They can track miles run, calories burned, and other fitness benchmarks and compare them to friends' progress, map routes, and a host of other running-related information.

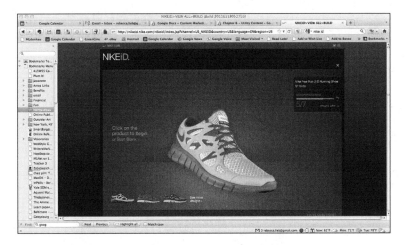

Figure 7.7 *Scratch that. I'd rather have the pink laces and the turquoise sole on my orange running shoes.*

These examples just scratch the surface of what must be hundreds of thousands of content-related utilities out there that bring people that much closer, for that much longer, with brands, products, and services. Utility content isn't the first resort of most content marketers. Generally, you'll need the help of developers or programmers to get an initiative off the ground. It's a somewhat more daunting prospect than writing an article or blog post or investing a small amount of money in a digital camera.

The barrier to entry is higher. But it's not much higher, and it's becoming easier every day. Moreover, as the digital environment increasingly shifts to mobile platforms such as smartphone and computers, it will become increasingly important to offer a degree of functionality (where's the nearest john?), not only information or entertainment.

What do your customers need to do, find, know, learn, or understand to get closer to your being able to fulfill their need? It's your job to figure that out and provide the utility to get them there.

> "What do your customers need to do, find, know, learn, or understand.... It's your job to figure that out."

8

Content Curation and Aggregation

What's the biggest problem marketers say they face when it comes to content marketing? Producing original content is the number one issue (73.6%), followed closely by finding the time to produce content (73.0%), according to the findings of a 2011 survey conducted by HiveFire (see Figure 8.1).

A study of business-to-business marketers conducted the previous year by Junta42 and MarketingProfs had similar findings (see Figure 8.2).

Small wonder. Consistently creating and publishing original content is a full-time job. It takes time, thought, and resources. That's why nearly half of marketing executives (48%) are using content curation according to a 2011 survey from HiveFire. And many more are aggregating content to publish on their blogs and websites and in social media outlets. As is shown in Figure 8.3, they're doing it to establish thought leadership (78.9%), to elevate brand visibility and generate buzz (76.1%), and encourage lead generation (60.6%).

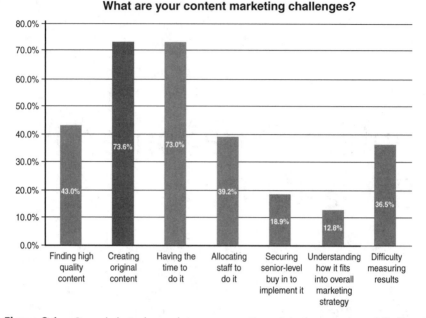

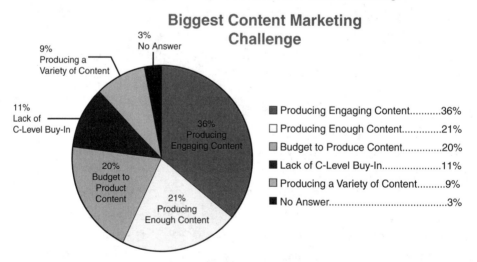

Figure 8.1   *Overwhelmingly, marketers say creating original content—and finding the time to do it—is their biggest challenge when it comes to content marketing.*

Figure 8.2   *To their credit, marketers don't just want to publish content for content's sake. They want it to resonate with their audience, which is no mean feat.*

Content curation and aggregation can be defined as a highly proactive and selective approach to finding, collecting, organizing, presenting, sharing, and displaying digital content around predefined sets of criteria and subject matter to appeal to a target audience. It's become essential not only to marketing and branding, but to journalism, reporting, and social media—often, it's a mashup of all these different and disparate channels.

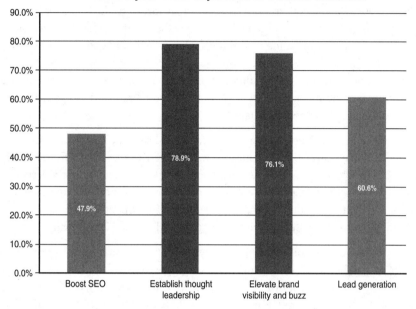

What are your main objectives of content curation?

Boost SEO	47.9%
Establish thought leadership	78.9%
Elevate brand visibility and buzz	76.1%
Lead generation	60.6%

Figure 8.3   *Research indicates there is a solid understanding of the benefits of strong content marketing: credibility, buzz, lead-generation, and search visibility.*

Why bother? Tons of reasons. It's a big, big web out there. There are literally billions of sites, millions of blogs, and more video being uploaded per minute to YouTube and tweets being tweeted than you could watch or read in a lifetime. The problem isn't enough content. It's knowing what content actually merits time and attention.

> "The problem isn't enough content. It's knowing what content actually merits time and attention."

More and more, people rely on trusted sources—friends, family, brands, companies, experts, you name it—to keep them informed, educated, and even amused. Just as you probably have one go-to friend for car advice, another who can tell you what new books or films are worth seeing, or another who's got the lowdown on the latest places to eat, business are collecting, organizing, and filtering content around their own fields of expertise.

Take bOINGbOING.net, one of the web's most popular blogs. Its traffic often exceeds that of NYTimes.com. The group blog is nothing more (or less) than curated content—items its contributors, and often its readers, find and share with others.

Content curation and aggregation can take many forms: feeds, "channels" (such as on YouTube), blogs, or even the links you upload to social media sites such as Facebook. It can be an online newsroom, a collection of links, an assortment of RSS feeds, or a Twitter list. Whatever form content curation does take, it's around a topic, a subject, or even a sensibility that speaks to the knowledge, expertise, taste, refinement, brand message, or persona of the person, brand, or company that has created the particular content channel.

Content channels can be as subject-specific as bee-keeping equipment or as amorphous as "what's cool." But they all serve multiple purposes, ranging from informing to engaging to entertaining. In an era where marketing is supplanting advertising and storytelling is an ever-more essential part of the marketing message, carefully curated content—well organized and presented—is an immense brand asset, be it to a humble, over-caffeinated individual blogger or a Fortune 100 company.

Curation and aggregation needn't be merely collecting and cataloging a bunch of links, abstracts, and headlines, of course. There's nothing wrong with writing up a brief paragraph or two putting your own spin on an external article or story, or blending outside content with your own original contributions. Pawan Deshpande, CEO of HiveFire, a company that makes a content curation tool, suggests a mix of perhaps 1 original piece per week plus 12 curated items of content. Your own mileage, of course, may vary.

Examples

Plenty of websites thrive with little to no original content. Google is a prime example. Search engines aggregate content from across the web; they publish little of their own. Travel sites such as Expedia and Kayak aggregate feeds from hundreds of hotels and airlines. Techmeme aggregates technology stories from across the web into one authoritative collection.

Of course, you can also apply this model to marketing. Purina's Pet Charts aggregates pet-related content from across the web (see Figure 8.4). GE's EcoPressed does the same thing with ecologically minded content, and Green Data News from Verne Global does much the same thing, but with a computer technology bent. Adobe's CMO.com is a collection of marketing stories and news targeted to this critical component of the company's target audience.

3M has a widget on its career page that contains articles highlighting the company's innovations and achievements, making it appear a more attractive place to work for job seekers. The tactic has also been embraced by the nonprofit sectors.

Organizations such as the Economic Development Council of Western Massachusetts have sites featuring content about business and economic growth in their region.

Of course, not all quality content is "out there." Many quality publications you might want to link to have content behind a paywall, such as with *The Wall Street Journal* or *The New York Times*. HiveFire CEO Pawan Deshpande doesn't see this as a significant barrier to publishing headlines, abstracts, or links to those pages. "We do have customers for whom almost all the content they aggregate is behind a paywall," he said, "Really, all they need to do is publish the abstract. Most of their clients have access to the full article."

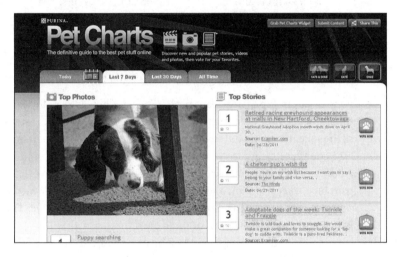

Figure 8.4 *Purina Pet Charts gathers pet-related content from around the world and places it in one spot for pet lovers.*

Curated content does more than augment websites, blogs, or social media channels. It can also be a great tactic to keep email newsletters interesting and relevant. The curated content you're using in online channels can be flowed into newsletters. Many marketers opt into services such as SmartBrief.com, a company that creates subject-specific newsletters created entirely of aggregated content. Their clients run the gamut and include thousands of B2B organizations and professional trade associations.

Finding Content

Curating and aggregating third-party content obviously requires less commitment on the creation side than does conjuring a steady stream of original content. Nevertheless, there's still a commitment of time, resources, and setting up procedures to mine and sift through sources.

Your first step is obvious: Scour the media and the Internet for topics of interest:

- Set up RSS feeds for keywords and phrases to automate delivery of web content from blogs, newswires, and news stories that is potentially of interest.

- Read relevant trade publications, newspapers, and magazines.

- Subscribe to trade organizations' and competitors' publications to spark new ideas.

  - Attend trade shows and conferences. Conference programmers are tasked with keeping current on industry trends and issues. Aside from conversations and learnings gleaned at these events, just keeping an eye on agendas can be a big tip-off.

  - Gather research and data, such as surveys, statistics, and reports. Mine numbers not only for potential sources of written content but also for visual ones: charts, graphs, and infographics.

  - Don't discount the mainstream news. Consider how larger stories might impact your own niche or vertical. The tragic, triple disaster of earthquake, tsunami, and nuclear catastrophe that struck Japan in 2011 could, for example, be a point of departure for content on a myriad of issues: disaster preparedness, construction, building inspection, insurance, energy policy, alternate power sources, emergency medical services, grief counseling, homelessness, and search and rescue. The list goes on and on, and each of these cited topics is rife with subtopics that might be relevant to a business's core competencies. Finding the relevant coverage and briefly adding a point of view or explanation of a relevant angle to your own target audience is a perfectly legitimate form of content curation.

Don't Be a Pirate

It should go without saying (but alas, too often it does not) that curating and aggregating content comes with a set of obligations—ethical and moral, as well as legal.

Respect copyright. Most editorial sites have published guidelines regarding the reuse of their content. In most (but certainly not all) cases, this can be summarized as allowing third parties to link to the full story or item with a headline and brief descriptive blurb or a quote of reasonable length. Most publishers are happy for the link. It increases both their traffic and their search engine visibility.

Other sites have more liberal or more restrictive policies. When in doubt, ask. Shoot over an email explaining what you'd like to use and why (supplying any necessary links to the site or channel). With websites getting the bulk of their traffic these days from third-party sites such as Facebook and Twitter, publishers are really beginning to understand the value of such referrals, and linking to content legally is much easier than it was in the days before social media when many publishers thought proprietary was the way to go.

Aggregation, Filtering, and Curation Platforms

Content aggregation and curation is only emerging as far as technology solutions are concerned. Some are newsletter specific, whereas others are aimed at communities or hyperlocal markets. Some emphasize SEO, whereas others lean on social filtering. Some work on your sites, whereas others create content sites on their own platforms. There are no cookie-cutter solutions, but there are technologies that help publishers and marketers aggregate, filter, curate, and publish content.

Here's a list of some commercial solutions:

- **Aggreage**—Creates topic-centered sites around specific market segments
- **CIThread**—Helps editors curate content for online communities
- **Curata**—HiveFire's content curation and distribution platform
- **CurationStation**—Web-based software service offering a tool kit for gathering/monitoring, selecting, and sharing specific items among dynamic content
- **DayLife**—Publisher platform that consolidates media sourcing, management, curation, and composition
- **Eqentia**—Enterprise platform for aggregating, curating, consuming, analyzing, and republishing news content
- **idio**—Platform for aggregation and publishing using semantic extraction and other analytics approaches
- **Loud3r**—A real-time content discovery, curation and publishing platform
- **MainStreetConnect**—Creates independent hyperlocal news publications
- **OneSpot**—Aggregates, filters, and prioritizes content
- **Outside.in**—Hyperlocal content solutions for sites and apps
- **Perfect Market**—Helps publishers identify, package, distribute, and monetize content
- **Publish2**—Content acquisition and workflow optimization

- **PublishThis**—On-demand content publishing platform for discovery, collection, and delivery of relevant, real-time content; provides audience segmentation capabilities

- **SmartBrief**—Industry- or topic-specific email newsletters

9

Finding a Voice

How you say it matters just as much as what you say.

So how do you go about finding the right "voice" with which to communicate through your content marketing efforts? If you've spent any time at all on social media sites or pondering content marketing, you know it's not the same one in which your wrote your senior thesis. It's also not your job interview voice, and it's not strict adherence to the reverse-pyramid AP style book.

Content marketing expert Patricia Redsicker provides a great example of the difference a voice can make in communication, content, and brand. "If I read an article on how to braise a chicken from Martha Stewart, I expect a formal, scholarly, exact approach. If I read Emeril Lagasse, I expect a casual approach, with recipe flexibility and punctuation—BAM!"

Neither Martha's nor Emeril's voices, cooking or recipe-wise, are "right" or "wrong." Instead, each is different, distinctive. It's their unique voices, approaches, and personalities that lend a certain caché to their recipes. Each stands out, and each has a broad and loyal following. Each also is recognizable and has a distinct personality; at the same time, each is clear and understandable.

What's critical here is that both have a vice that's not only inextricably linked with their respective identities, but also defines the way they relate to their respective audiences, and their audiences (in turn) to them. One's a somewhat prim and correct—and very feminine—Connecticut Yankee hostess; the other's an earthy, informal, and somewhat macho 'Nawlins native. Each voice reflects not only personality, but also product and brand, complete with taglines. ("BAM!" and "It's a good thing.")

Each is effectively defined by a voice that's human and genuine. Those two qualities should form the basis of the way content addresses an online audience.

Here are a few things an online voice should not sound like:

- A formal newspaper article
- Edward R. Murrow
- A legal brief
- An instruction manual
- Your senior thesis
- A sales brochure
- A commercial

These formats—and their attendant voices—aren't bad in and of themselves. However, when you are creating online content—whether in written text or spoken word—you should make an effort to strike a more informal, conversational tone with the audience. To some this comes easily. It's second nature. For others, it's more difficult to strike the right balance.

For this latter group, it may help to write the way you talk (rather than the way you usually write). Imagine you're sitting down with a customer or a prospect, or even talking to a friend about your business, products, or services. You likely speak with animated passion and enthusiasm. You speak conversationally and in all probability, much more informally than you'd write what you're actually saying. You strive to create a bond with the person (or people) you're addressing, to encourage their interest and willingness to engage. You're concerned less with being formally "correct" than you are with really communicating on an engaging, personal level—with creating an emotional bond.

You also would adopt your voice for the channel. You'd be more formal in a whitepaper than in, say, a tweet in which, limited to 140 characters or less, you'd have no problem resorting to common social media abbreviations (LOL!).

Spokesperson or Spokes-Character

This technique isn't for every business, but some organizations have found great success in creating a character that clearly represents its online voice. We've already seen plenty of cases, mostly in online video, in which these characters are real people: Wine Library's Gary Vaynerchuk, for example, or Blendtec's Tom Dickson.

But taking a page from traditional marketing's tried-and-true spokescharacter concept: The Pillsbury Doughboy, the Geico Gekko, Madge the Manicurist, Mrs. Folger, or Mr. Clean (to name but a few) online spokes-characters work well for some as representatives of the overall brand—and brand voice.

A stellar example is the fictitious Emma. She even has a company named after her. MyEmma.com is the domain of Emma Email Marketing, a brand organized around Emma.

Figure 9.1   *MyEmma.com.*

Who's Emma? "We all are," states the company website, next to a photo of the entire staff. The About Us page goes on to explain, "Sure, it's a nice and handy abbreviation of the phrase email marketing, but more importantly, it brings with it an inherent human quality. It's a real name—like Antoinette or Frederick, only shorter."

Emma is personified on the site by a cartoon drawing of an intelligent-looking young woman. (She wears glasses, after all.) The company isn't trying to convince you it has an actual Emma at a real desk somewhere. Rather, Emma is a state of mind and a tone of voice who can authoritatively, yet with humor and intelligence, address your email marketing needs. Here's how she talks about her clients:

"More than 30,000 fine organizations around the world use Emma to power their email campaigns and surveys. And though they have different brands, goals, and opinions on the best Hall and Oates song, they all share a common desire to bring style, ease, and success to their marketing and communication efforts."

Such examples date back to the beginning of dot-com businesses. Who doesn't remember the Pets.com sock puppet, who lived an afterlife longer than the company that the floppy mascot represented?

"When you can sell your advertising at retail, that's a sure sign of success."

Travelocity's Roaming Gnome, first used in a 2004 ad campaign, has become that company's de facto mascot, as shown in Figure 9.2. (Fans can even now buy a replica gnome on Amazon.com. When you can sell your advertising at retail, that's a sure sign of success.)

Figure 9.2 *Not only can this gnome find great travel deals, but he can also give you pointers on safe and fun travel!*

In intervening years, the gnome, who speaks with a distinct accent—talk about voice—has had his own (now defunct) website, tweets, has appeared in two feature films, has Facebook and MySpace profiles, and is inextricably linked with the brand he represents. He's also a primary voice for Travelocity.

Another online travel company, Priceline.com, has its own high-profile voice in the person of William Shatner. Infamous as Captain James T. Kirk, the intrepid voyager from *Star Trek*, there's definitely a travel link between the spokesperson and the brand. In this case, Shatner-as-spokesperson represents just one of many examples of the celebrity spokesperson, another opportunity for developing a voice this book would be remiss if it were to overlook.

Figure 9.3   *He's no longer guiding the Starship Enterprise, but he can steer you to good travel deals.*

Celebrities can accord many benefits to brands, which is why many of their voices have been interchangeable with brand voices for decades. Online, it's no different— only the channels are. For tens of thousands of dollars, the irritating Kardashian sisters or Paris Hilton might consider tweeting on your behalf.

Of course, once you're enlisting a *paid* spokesperson, you're very much on the verge of advertising rather than practicing content marketing. That, of course, is beyond the purview of this book.

10

Overview of Digital Content Channels

"The right time to get on board is when you have a well-conceived reason to leverage the channel."

Websites, microsites, ebooks, social media, blogs...the list of potential digital content marketing channels is enormous and only growing as technological innovations create new ways for regular people and marketers alike to create, showcase, and disseminate content.

All have advantages and disadvantages, different barriers to entry, different audience and targeting potential, and varying benefits dependent on needs, focus, and target audience. Most marketers will find that a mix of channels suits their needs. But which channels, and in what proportion?

The only way to find out is to experiment and to test— not randomly, of course, but based on defined goals, strategies, and needs. It's the old stick-a-toe-in-the-water- and-see-what-works approach. Don't be afraid to start small and even to fail—provided you learn from your mistakes. Some initiatives work better than others. Some may fall flat. Keep an open and creative mind; perhaps the type of content you're publishing on one channel isn't working there but might succeed elsewhere, perhaps in another form.

Perhaps the most critical point to bear in mind is that all these channels are tools. They're a means to an end, and that end comprises both your strategy and your goals. "We need a Facebook page!" (or whatever the channel du jour happens to be) is a call that's been echoing for far too long in far too many marketing meetings. Maybe you do need a Facebook page. Maybe you don't. Just because all the other kids are doing it doesn't mean you have to, too. The right time to get on board is when you have a well-conceived reason to leverage the channel, not simply because it's there.

This chapter provides an overview of the major digital content channels. This list isn't intended to be exhaustive, but rather to explore all the major categories and channels out there to provide a bird's-eye view of them, including their benefits and limitations and the purposes they're best suited for.

Social Networks

Defined by Wikipedia as "a social structure made up of individuals (or organizations) called "nodes," which are tied (connected) by one or more specific types of interdependency, such as friendship, kinship, common interest, financial exchange, dislike, sexual relationships, or relationships of beliefs, knowledge or prestige," social networks are far more familiar these days by their brand names, such as Facebook, Google+, or MySpace.

Facebook

Description:

If you don't know Facebook, well, where have you been? With over half a billion users, if Facebook were a country, it would be the third-biggest one on the planet. Its current U.S. audience is estimated by eMarketer to exceed 132 million users and is expected to rise to more than 152 million by 2013. Among teens and younger users, penetration is greater than 80% and will be nearing 90% in a couple years' time.

Facebook, in short, is *the* online mass media channel, not just the leader in social networking, as illustrated in Figure 10.1. According to Mashable, users spend more time on Facebook than on Google, Yahoo, YouTube, Microsoft, Wikipedia, and Amazon—combined.

> "Facebook, in short, is *the* online mass media channel, not just the leader in social networking."

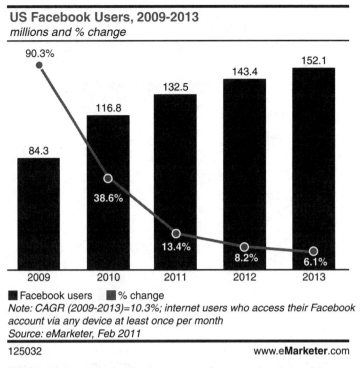

US Facebook Users, 2009-2013
millions and % change

- ■ Facebook users   ■ % change
- *Note: CAGR (2009-2013)=10.3%; internet users who access their Facebook account via any device at least once per month*
- *Source: eMarketer, Feb 2011*

125032   www.**eMarketer**.com

Figure 10.1 *Facebook's growth over the past few years has been phenomenal. By 2010, its population made it big enough to qualify as the world's third-largest country – if Facebook were a country.*

Pros:

- Opportunities to cultivate a network of people, as well as fans of brands, companies, products, services, and events.

- Disseminating news feeds and updates, and creating the option for users to share these with their own personal networks.

- Sharing content. Facebook feeds and shared links can really boost traffic to external websites. Promoting blog posts and tweets on Facebook is a way to bring messages to a broader audience that may not be following your messaging in other channels.

- Engagement and feedback. Wall posts create a dialogue with users, friends, and fans, offering marketers an opportunity to be reactive as well as proactive in terms of content. Topical discussion can be incredibly effective in this arena. In 2010, Greenpeace launched a page on

Facebook that was highly critical of Nestlé's environmental practices that were threatening orangutan habitats. The pile-on was enormous, prompting Nestlé to radically change its environmental practices (see Figure 10.2).

Figure 10.2   *Nestle made radical changes to its environmental practices after Greenpeace was critical of Nestle on Facebook.*

- Multimedia. Facebook's platform encompasses content in all its forms: written words, graphics, audio, video, and interactive apps and games.

- Increasing business-to-business (B2B) usage. Originally, Facebook was viewed as a marketing channel primarily by large consumer brands that leveraged the fun factor. The user base is now so universal that B2B marketers have become equally at home in the environment.

Cons:

- Facebook's privacy policy limits the metrics and data available to page administrators. Don't expect the depth and breadth of reporting you'd get in a web analytics tool.

User Base:

Companies, brands, products, services, events, cause marketing, and individuals make up the user base. Facebook fans pages run the gamut from toilet paper brands (really) to business conferences. The extremely large audience and wide range of tools and features have made it a de facto marketing platform for nearly everyone and everything.

LinkedIn

Description:

LinkedIn is the largest global professional social network. It allows individual users to showcase professional and academic experience and to connect with current and former colleagues and thus to research prospects and leads through connections' connections. The site also features Company Profile pages.

Pros:

LinkedIn is all about professional networking: recruiting, job-hunting, and lead generation. In addition to cultivating a personal brand, company profile pages create opportunities for marketers to positively position their organizations. This can be done with basic company information, lists of products and services, a "follow company" feature, and the ability to update Company Profile pages with news feeds, tweets, blog entries, and multimedia content (the latter with a premium paid account), primarily for recruitment and lead-generation purposes.

Cons:

Company profile pages require a sole administrator.

User base:

Recruiters, job hunters, sourcing, and lead-generation make up the user base.

Google+

Description:

Among social networks, Google+ is very much the new kid on the block, having launched in late June 2011. As with nearly everything that Google launches, the buzz was intense, and the clamor to get an invitation to join was nearly deafening. Heralded as a "content sharing" platform, Google+ makes it easy to share all types of content. It's most differentiating feature is empowering users to answer the question: Share what with whom?

Unlike Facebook and LinkedIn, where users share with their entire networks, Google+ encourages segmentation into "circles." Users can have groups of co-workers, friends, family, baseball fans, fishing buddies— anything they can think of that's relevant. After all, that thrash metal video you want to share with your friends in the dorm isn't necessarily something you want Grandma to click on. Google understands this.

Although Google has opened the platform to the public, it's still on the fence about letting brands, companies, products and other nonhuman entities on to the platform. At launch, the Ford Motor Company was the *only* brand on the platform. It remains to be seen what features will roll out on Google+ in general, and more specifically, what marketers and commercial entities can and can't do on the platform.

Pros:

Segmentation, the "circles" feature, will be critically valuable to marketers who take the time to use the feature judiciously. Companies can segment followers by product group, or separate customers from investors, for example. Additionally, followers can be segmented as customers, prospects, or into different geographical areas.

All search results are personalized to some degree, even if you're not signed in to a Google account. (For example, Google will deliver results based on the geographic information in your device's IP address.) Google+ followers become part of a social circle, and their content will rank higher in search results as a result (see Figure 10.3). If you follow Ford on Google+ and the company shares content relevant to a search you perform on Google, that result gets pushed up in search results and highlighted on the search results page, as shown in Figure 10.4.

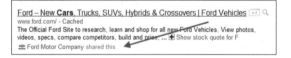

Figure 10.3 *Connecting the dots— Google Search prioritizes results based on who you're connected with on Google+.*

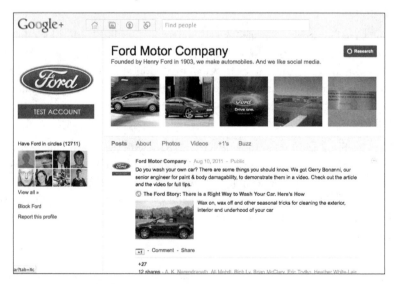

Figure 10.4 *When Google+ launched, it allowed only one brand on the network: the Ford Motor Company.*

Huddles is a feature allowing up to 10 people to have a private chat on the platform. There's potential for mini-webinars, analyst calls, and a degree of customer service in this feature.

The Sparks feature allows content found as the result of a search to be shared with one click—no copying or pasting required to share with a network.

Cons:

The biggest disadvantage at present is Google+ is still very limited in terms of what brands, products, or indeed any commercial entity can do with the platform. It's coming, but Google typically takes its time rolling out new features. Watch this space.

Another question mark, at least as far as marketers are concerned, is the increased privacy features in Google+. Although obviously a boon for users, particularly in light of the flack Facebook has taken for its privacy policies, Google+ conceals as much as it reveals. What circles a user has, who or how many people are in them, the size of their network—that's all privileged information. The fact that this information is private calls into question how much analytics data will be available, and how valuable it will be, after Google+ is more broadly available as a brand platform. Again, the jury's still out, which perhaps is the biggest drawback of all. Still, it's no reason not to begin testing the Google+ waters now.

User Base:

Google+ is the fastest-growing social network in history. Google has an enormous user base, and thanks to Facebook, they're well acquainted with social networks. In its first two weeks, Google+ already had 10 million registered users, a number that continues to grow rapidly.

Custom Social Networks

Description

A number of white-label platforms such as Ning, SocialGO, rSitez, and INgage provide tools to create custom social networks for enterprise, government, special interest groups, and other like-minded individuals.

 Note

A white label platform is a social network community based on a generic framework created by a third-party developer. Unlike Facebook or LinkedIn, which use custom frameworks they created from scratch, some social networks use a generic template as a more cost-effective means of creating their networks.

Pros:

These platforms can be highly customized and afford a degree of privacy, exclusivity, and community that exceeds public social networks such as Facebook—assuming that's what's desired. The private platforms are also ad free, but of course they come with a cost. Many offer branded tools, such as custom media players, and most integrate with existing social media sharing sites such as Flickr and YouTube. Many companies cultivate research panels, which they run on these platforms. Because they're not broadly public, an exclusive feeling of real community can result.

Cons:

Although custom social networks are rich in features, they require more thought and resources dedicated to design and implementation, as well as to cultivating members. Because they're not part of broader social networks, custom networks lack the "halo" effect of easily allowing content to be shared across networks of friends.

User Base:

All sorts of organizations, from bands cultivating their fan base to professional interest groups (such as email marketers), leverage these platforms to showcase content, disseminate news and information, and demonstrate thought leadership.

Geo-Social Networks

Description:

Geo-social networks (the two biggies are Foursquare and Gowalla, although Facebook and Yelp are also players in the space) are location-aware mobile platforms that allow users to "check in" to locations: bars, restaurants, work, sporting, or cultural events—wherever they happen to be. Depending on the service, they can see if networked friends are present, read tips or take advantage of special offers at the location (perhaps free beer if it's your first check-in), or earn badges or points for the number or nature of the places they visit.

Pros:

Geo-social networks encourage users to review the places they visit as well as leave tips for their friends. ("Order the burger with the special sauce!") They encourage exploration of localities, encourage peer-to-peer recommendations, and venues public relations (PR) and promotional opportunities. Increasingly, users are encouraged to upload photos of venues along with reviews and tips. Large brands are beginning to find new ways to leverage the platforms. For example, at a recent New York Auto Show, Foursquare subscribers could check in to the event and then show a Mercedes-Benz rep their phone's screen in exchange for a $1,000 voucher toward a new set of (still-pricey) wheels.

Cons:

These networks are relatively new, having been around less than five years. Adoption is still relatively small—at present, geo-social networks are limited to relatively young, tech-savvy users who own smartphones.

User Base:

At present, mostly local businesses—butchers, bakers, candlestick-makers, restaurants, hair salons, bars, shops, pizzerias, and dry cleaners. If you run a business with a retail or walk-in presence, consider promotions, and encourage your clientele to boost your visibility in these channels. This counts for national chains, too, of course. Franchises such as Starbucks and Walgreens are leveraging the channels. So are media companies such as the History Channel and *The Wall Street Journal* that encourage and reward check-ins at, respectively, historical or Wall Street locations that are relevant to the brands.

Location-Based Content

Description:

Like geo-social networks, location-based content is delivered to mobile devices based on the location of that device. Although, like Foursquare or Gowalla, the content can be tied to a social network, location-based content isn't necessarily social.

A highly sophisticated example of location-based content is NearbyNow. This is a service that's been available primarily to participating shopping malls over the past several years. Tell it you're looking for men's Ralph Lauren jeans, size 36, in black, and it will shoot back real-time information regarding the nearest retailer that currently has that item in stock. Inventory is updated every 24 hours, and customers can place a reserve on a particular item.

Location-based content needn't be that sophisticated. Geo-tagging businesses and photographs is enough to make them pinpointable on a map. QR codes (block-shaped bar codes) can deliver specific local information (see Figure 10.5). In fact, Google Local has been encouraging local merchants to display free QR codes in their windows. Snap one with a mobile device, and information displayed could range from sales and specials to opening hours, contact information, and even photos of the interior. An exceptionally wide variety of providers, ranging from Google Maps to Yelp to Aircell (a wireless provider in India), offer mobile users ways to find the nearest drugstore, pizza, or gym (see Figure 10.6).

Figure 10.5   *A QR code is a type of bar code readable by smartphones and other mobile devices. Scan one and information is delivered straight to your phone or tablet.*

Custom location-based content applications are another option. The North Carolina State University campus offers maps, event listings and promotions, reviews, photo sharing, and rewards schemes such as Foursquare-style badges and points for checking in to specific locations or campus events (see Figure 10.6).

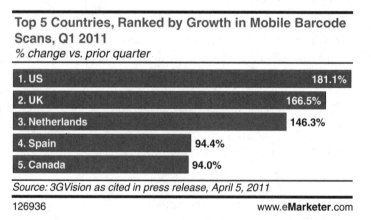

Top 5 Countries, Ranked by Growth in Mobile Barcode Scans, Q1 2011
% change vs. prior quarter

1. US	181.1%
2. UK	166.5%
3. Netherlands	146.3%
4. Spain	94.4%
5. Canada	94.0%

Source: 3GVision as cited in press release, April 5, 2011

126936   www.**eMarketer**.com

Figure 10.6   *The United States is a growing market in terms of actual use of mobile barcodes, or QR codes. European and Asian countries aren't experiencing the same degree of growth as we are here because they're already well accustomed to scanning codes on products and in print media Fourteen million Americans scanned QR codes with their mobile phones in June, 2011, according to comScore.*

Figure 10.7 *Scan a barcode at North Carolina State University and get all the campus goings-on—right on your mobile device.*

Pros:

Location-based content has immediate contextual relevance. It's linked to the here and now, whether offering enhanced information, guidance, rewards, incentives to purchase, or answers to questions. It helps connect places to people and people to the places they visit, and it can provide influence at just the right moment.

Cons:

Location-based content works only on smartphones and tablet computers (such as the iPad or Galaxy Tab). The good news is that adoption of these platforms is on a healthy upswing. Adoption of location-based services will lag slightly behind adoption of these technology platforms. And often, visitors may need visual, onsite reminders (such as signage, leaflets, or prominently placed QR codes) that location-based information is invisibly floating all around them, waiting to be invited onto their handheld screens.

User Base:

As with geo-social networks, location-based information is for organizations with a "there" there. Stores and restaurants are a given. Also think large, complex installations such as malls, theme parks, museums; airports, train stations, and similar travel

> "Location-based content has immediate contextual relevance. It's linked to the here and now."

hubs; as well as campuses, both academic and corporate. Cities or municipalities could do well branding, promoting and identifying distinctive regions or areas with location-based content. Think major parks or recreation areas, the French Quarter in New Orleans, Times Square or Greenwich Village in New York City, or areas considered to be the restaurant, shopping, museum, or gallery districts of their towns.

Online Directories

Description:

Directories are, well, directories—and there are more of them online than you can shake a stick at. They range from Wikipedia to DMOZ to industry, city, and country-specific listings of businesses by vertical, location…what have you. Zagat.com is a restaurant directory, Martindale Hubbell is a directory of attorneys, and Thomas.net lists industrial suppliers. There's an online directory for just about everything.

Pros:

Directories are the basic building blocks of content marketing. They get you "out there," listed and visible in places where people seek information about you—or organizations that are very much like you. Directory listings are a great and funda-mental way to boost search engine visibility. They build credibility by virtue of inclusion. Approached strategically, they can make organizations prominent in cat-egories other than their main vertical. Take, for example, New York's Museum of Modern Art (MoMA). It's primarily a museum, of course, and would appear in list-ings for New York sightseeing, cultural institutions, and so on. A judicious use of directories, however, can also boost inclusion in directories for categories such as gift shops, cinemas, and restaurants—all part of MoMA's core offerings and major sources of revenue for the institution.

Cons:

Cons for online directories are nonexistent, really. There's no reason not to make an effort to be included in any relevant directory.

User Base:

Every business, organization, product, or service makes up the user base. It's also per-fectly reasonable to view social networks such as LinkedIn and Facebook as "people directories" and use them accordingly, for personal branding and networking.

Email

Description:

C'mon—obviously, you know what email is! But it's likely you haven't considered all the content marketing opportunities inherent in the channel.

Email newsletters? A given, of course. But even email messages your organization sends contains content: press releases, news alerts, order confirmations, event updates, new product announcements, and reminders. All these messages are opportunities to create content that's compelling, engaging, and beneficial to both your brand and the audience you're addressing. Emails can also contain links, of course, and drive traffic to other content channels on your website or elsewhere.

Pros:

Adhering to email best practices and sending only messages to people who have explicitly opted-in to receive them means you already have a relationship with whomever you're messaging. In theory, this means they want to hear from you; they're receptive to your messages.

Cons:

Inbox fatigue is a real issue. It's harder now, but hardly impossible, to build opt-in lists without providing real value to subscribers and recipients. A solid email strategy therefore requires more effort, creativity, and hard work than it did, say, 10 years ago.

User Base:

Because existing customers and prospects expect most organizations they do business with to communicate via email, an email content strategy is essential for most businesses.

Blogs

Description:

The word "blog" is short for "weblog." Blogs are publishing platforms that create a website that displays entries in reverse-chronological order. Essentially, the underlying technology of a blog is an all-in-one content management system. In addition to capabilities for posting multimedia content and syndicating content via RSS feeds, the majority of blogs are interactive, allowing readers to comment on entries. Blogs have become exceedingly popular, both for professional and personal bloggers. According to Wikipedia, by early 2011 there were more than 156 million publicly accessible blogs on the Web.

Pros:

Blogs are the hub of countless organizations' content marketing efforts. They can establish thought leadership; quickly and easily share news and developments; offer commentary on industry, news, or relevant trends; and become a continual source of two-way conversation between a company and its audience. They have the potential to increase media coverage and relationships with influences, and blog posts can easily flow into and feed additional content channels such as social networks, video-sharing sites, Twitter, and the like to create additional reach. Blogs can also function as a customer service vehicle. Are sales or tech support staff constantly asked the same questions? Address them on the blog. And because blog platforms are optimized for search, blogs can contribute enormously to boosting organic search engine rankings.

No topic or industry is too arcane for a blog. Don't believe it? Consider Indium, which publishes no less than 73 different blogs…on soldering materials! Entries are translated into seven languages. Why 73 blogs? That's how many keywords the company's marketing communications director Rick Short identified as terms that prospects search on when seeking the products and services the company offers.

"My goal is to generate opt-in, self-qualified, preferably urgent customer contact," said Short. "When we implemented, our contact rate increased 600% overall. We link to the blogs from everything we do: speaking, whitepapers, and the website. Content to contact to cash. That's my leg of the race. Contact is my number. It's about lead generation. It's going so well, we're now generating far too many leads for our current system to handle."

Figure 10.8 shows an example of Indium's blogs.

Figure 10.8   *Indium's blogs prove that no topic is too esoteric for a one blog…or 73 blogs!*

Cons:

Blogging is not for the unenthusiastic or noncommittal. How often to post, or what to post, is an ongoing issue that requires careful planning and dedication. This stick-to-itiveness applies not only to blogging per se, but to keeping up with industry news and trends, responding to comments, developing an editorial calendar, and tracking visitor trends and metrics over time. As advantageous as a robust, frequently updated blog can be, a derelict, abandoned, or flabby blog also speaks volumes about the organization behind it.

User Base:

Blogs should be targeted to a specific audience: for instance, clients, customers, prospects, the media, or influencers. Blogs can even be a form of internal communication and information dissemination. Only by approaching blogging strategically and defining those audiences and their needs can you determine the focus of a blog—or multiple blogs, as the case may be. Some organizations may elect to run multimedia blogs, whereas others run video blogs or podcasts, which is really audio blogging.

Figure 10.9 shows the results of an eMarketer study into the top reasons some companies launched a corporate blog.

> "As advantageous as a robust, frequently updated blog can be, a derelict, abandoned, or flabby blog also speaks volumes about the organization behind it."

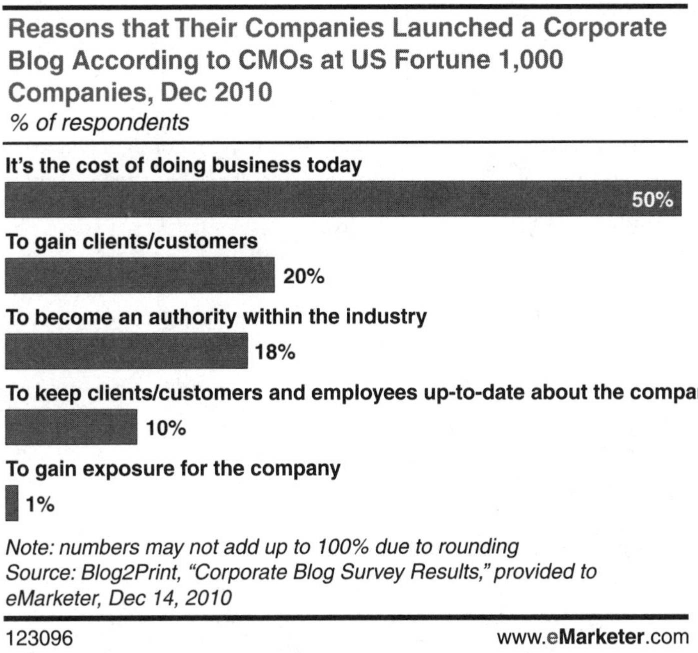

Reasons that Their Companies Launched a Corporate Blog According to CMOs at US Fortune 1,000 Companies, Dec 2010
% of respondents

It's the cost of doing business today

50%

To gain clients/customers

20%

To become an authority within the industry

18%

To keep clients/customers and employees up-to-date about the company

10%

To gain exposure for the company

1%

Note: numbers may not add up to 100% due to rounding
Source: Blog2Print, "Corporate Blog Survey Results," provided to eMarketer, Dec 14, 2010

123096   www.eMarketer.com

Figure 10.9   *Half of those polled said their corporate blog is just part of the cost of doing business. Source: eMarketer.*

Social Bookmarking

Description:

Services such as Delicious, Digg, and StumbleUpon (the biggies), as well as others including AddThis, Diigo, and ShareThis, turn bookmarking a web page (that is, piece of content) into something social. Other users can see what you've bookmarked, add your bookmarks to their collections, and tag and organize bookmarks, making them, in turn, visible to more users. Many services let users annotate or comment on bookmarks, as well as subscribe to collections, so they're notified when new links are added. User groups can be private, within a predefined network, or wholly public.

Pros:

The act of bookmarking a piece of content—these days, usually from an embedded button on the web page itself—is akin to voting for it. By boosting a piece of content's visibility in social bookmarking services, you're boosting its visibility and searchability, tagging, and organizing to make it easier to find, and you're encouraging others to do the same.

Cons:

Cons are few for social bookmarking. Obviously, to keep social bookmarking fresh and lively, it helps to have content to share (either original or aggregated) and to have someone administrate both the bookmarking as well as the tagging/organizational part of the program.

User Base:

Organizations that want to boost sharing and dissemination of content make up the user base.

Online Video

Description:

Video sharing websites in which users can upload and share videos, either within the site itself or by using the service as a server that allows videos to easily be embedded on blogs, web pages, and so on. Google-owned YouTube is the 600-pound gorilla in this space, but Vimeo is a strong contender for higher resolution video. Video can also be uploaded to other platforms, of course, ranging from Facebook to your own website, but the ability to share and embed media on other platforms is then lost or greatly diminished.

Pros:

Once an expensive and highly technical proposition, hosting and sharing video content is becoming even easier than creating it. If a picture is worth a thousand words, a video can be worth thousands more than that, deepening engagement, offering visual how-tos, providing entertainment—you name it. Video sharing affords all sorts of benefits, such as creating custom channels on sharing sites and offering rich metrics and analytics, particularly on YouTube, which integrates Google Analytics. Search engine optimization (SEO) is also a benefit, particularly for video content that is well labeled, titled, tagged, and often, accompanied by a transcript of spoken-word content. Additionally, YouTube is immensely global; it's available in 14 languages and 21 countries.

Cons:

Although you can shoot video with a cameraphone, you'll likely want a slightly more polished look for business content, so an upfront investment is most likely required for a decent camera, tripod, lighting, and so on. You'll probably also want to look into basic editing capabilities so you can add music, titles, and more. All in all, this probably isn't a significant monetary investment, but it requires a certain level of technical know-how to look moderately professional. Also, unless you invest in a branded YouTube channel, third-party ads can appear on your content.

User Base:

Anyone can be a potential audience member for an online video. A marketer's ability to leverage video content is limited only by their imagination. TV spots can live on in perpetual life online. Video can serve as how-to content, executives can be interviewed, product features can be highlighted and shown off—you name it. Online shoe retailer Zappos has uploaded more than 58,000 short videos of its staff (not professional models) showing off the shoes, bags, and clothes it sells. It found that when a product page includes a video explanation, not only do purchases rise, but also returns decrease. So effective is the strategy that the company is currently pumping out some 400 new short videos per day (see Figure 10.10).

Video can also serve as a means of extending a popular promotion. In 2010, Friskies cat food released a popular ad called "Adventureland," featuring a cat on a trippy, psychedelic journey through an animated fantasy landscape (see Figure 10.11). So popular was the spot on YouTube (it also screened on television and in movie theatres) that the company rereleased the ad a year later with a modified ending. Friskies hopes to recapture the audience who had become fans of its content and helped to spread it.

Figure 10.10   *Zappos posts about 400—yes, 400—short video clips like this one, every single day.*

Figure 10.11   *One far-out kitty.*

Podcasts

Description:

Think of podcasts as radio shows to go. A podcast is a digital audio file, playable on computers, tablets, and portable media devices such as MP3 players and smartphones. Podcasts are most often distributed via RSS feeds or over Apple's iTunes platform.

Pros:

Podcasts can be a great way to connect with customers on handheld devices—think jogging or drive time or downtime. Because the two primary distribution methods— RSS feeds and iTunes—make it easy to subscribe to podcasts, they can be a high-tech way to continually reach an audience daily, weekly, monthly, or whatever the schedule is. Although podcasts can be produced with a high level of sophistication, they can also be a great communication medium for people who are more comfortable speaking than they are writing or perhaps appearing on-camera. Podcasts are also easily and effectively integrated into blogs.

Cons:

Although some companies such as Accenture offer what they term "video podcasts," they aren't podcasts at all. They're YouTube videos. Real podcasts have no visual content, which can be a drawback for some. Audiences need a small degree of technical savviness to download, subscribe to, and listen to a podcast. Metrics can be mushy if you're measuring the effect of a podcast program or initiative. You can count subscriptions and downloads of podcasts, but it's not possible to know how many episodes were actually listened to or how much of the content was heard.

User Base:

Podcasts work for all types of content, from entertainment to instructional and how-to type information. Like radio programming, podcasts are episodic and consistent in nature. Determine a frequency and a theme and stick to both.

Webinars

Description:

If you've ever attended a lecture or a conference seminar in which a speaker delivers a talk while running through a slideshow or PowerPoint presentation, you've been to the nondigital version. Put the presentation online and *voilà*—it's a webinar. Slide-by-slide visuals are accompanied by the speaker's live audio presentation.

Pros:

One major plus is that you can reach a broad and geographically disparate audience without having to worry about travel and other expenses, such as renting a hall or feeding and watering the audience. All webinar software enables interactive Q&A so that in addition to providing informational and/or complex content, audience members can individually ask questions for which they receive tailored responses from the speakers. Additionally, because most webinars require attendees to register, the resulting email list can provide opportunities to follow up with potential leads in the form of email, whitepapers, ebooks, and so on.

Cons:

As with virtually any slideshow lecture, webinars are infinitely more suited to instructional and complex informational content. You'd have to be something akin to a comic genius to entertain or amuse in this channel. Webinars are also for relatively complex information. Generally lasting half an hour to an hour in duration, they're not for presenting simple concepts that can be covered in a one-page instructional sheet, for example. You'll also need a long list of prospects to attract a substantial enough audience to a webinar. To mitigate this, many companies partner with publishers, media companies, or professional associations to leverage their lists for invitations (for a fee). Lots of aggressive marketing is required to build an audience, even for a free webinar.

User Base:

Webinars are for companies with products or services that require a learning curve, high degree of consideration, new technology, or other factors requiring education and explanation.

Twitter (and Microblogging)

Description:

Twitter is a lot like blogging, only it's much smaller and faster. Tweets are limited to 140 characters, so messages must be super-compacted. Because they're broadcast (and indexed by search engines) in near real-time, Twitter is a lightening-fast channel.

Pros:

Companies leverage Twitter for all types of messaging. Dell has raked in millions offering sales and special deals to its Twitter followers (see Figure 10.12). Jet Blue, American Express, and Comcast use the channel largely to address customer service issues and to monitor customer concerns. It's not only about what you broadcast, Twitter is an excellent tool to monitor conversations that are occurring around brands, products, companies, and their services—both positive and negative. Twitter is also a great way to direct people to deeper content on the Web: blog posts, articles, videos, and the like, via links in tweets. And tweets can be retweeted, bringing messages to broader audiences who may not follow your tweetstream but who follow those who follow you. This helps to build and widen your audience.

Cons:

Clearly, any message limited to a scant 140 characters is not going to be deep and complex. Messaging that's too sales-y or pitch-y or self-interested won't attract followers or fans. And while Twitter has grown exponentially in use over recent years, it's not useful for reaching audiences who are uninvolved in the channel.

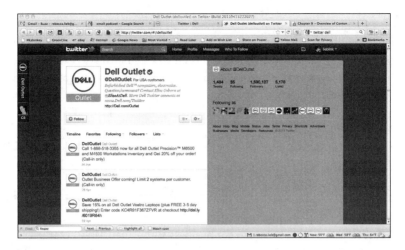

Figure 10.12   *Dell has turned Twitter into a hugely profitable channel by offering special deals to its followers.*

User Base:

Companies that want to quickly draw attention to content, monitor conversations about themselves online, and respond to those conversations are part of the user base. Publicly addressing customer services issues on Twitter is an indication that you care. Twitter can also serve as a rapid response system to address breaking news or time-sensitive issues and point followers to deeper information elsewhere on the Web.

Tumblr and Posterous

Description:

It should be mentioned that other platforms fall under the rubric "microblogging" without being Twitter. Tumblr and Posterous are two examples of blog platforms suitable for quickie posts of text or photos.

Pros:

Tumblr and Posterous have seen pickup in industries such as fashion. Kate Spade, for example, has a Tumblr blog that's essentially a notebook of aesthetic moments, from a perfectly formed cappuccino to a swatch of a particularly fetching shade of orange. Of course, occasional product shots are interspersed, but salesmanship is kept to a minimum. The blog is more about the brand's sensibility.

Cons:

Although microblogging platforms such as Tumblr and Posterous are dead simple to use, they're not as fully featured and flexible as "regular" blog platforms. You won't have as much freedom with design and formatting, for example, and you can't host the blog on your own server.

Long-Form Publishing (ebooks, Whitepapers, Digital Magazines)

Description:

Long-form publishing in the form of ebooks and whitepapers provides informative and educational content, primarily for business-to-business (B2B) marketers, tech companies, and other businesses that need to educate prospects on relatively complex products and services. Digital magazines work in both B2B and B2C marketing initiatives as they lend themselves more to the type of content that can be entertaining and immersive, as well as informative. They can even accommodate video and audio content, as does KLM's digital magazine *iFly*, which is also available in multiple languages (see Figure 10.13).

Figure 10.13   *KLM's digital magazine is a beautifully designed, multimedia version of the in-flight magazine You won't find it in the seat pocket in front of you, unless that's where you stashed your laptop.*

Pros:

These channels are used primarily for lead generation and thought-leadership. Although whitepapers are generally in PDF format, digital magazines and ebooks lend themselves to a variety of formats and platforms, including tablet computing and ebook readers (such as Kindle and Nook) and can be lavishly embellished with graphics, photos, charts, and diagrams. All are appropriate for deep information with companies that have ideas and concepts to disseminate. And because all these channels are essentially digital adoptions of traditional print formats, they are highly economical when compared to the cost of actually printing and distributing the content in physical formats. Moreover, multimedia content is an option. You can track downloads for whitepapers and eBooks. With digital magazines, richer metrics are available such as time spend, pages viewed, and so on.

Not to mention business results. Eloqua has, within two quarters, attributed $2.5 million in closed business to prospects who first downloaded one of the company's ebooks (see Figure 10.14). Another $4 million is in the active buying process, according to the company.

Cons:

Distribution strategies must be carefully conceived for all long-form content channels. Marketers hoping to capture too much user data from potential downloaders of their ebooks and whitepapers could be disappointed with results if they require too much data before allowing the content to be downloaded. Long-form content that's viewed on screens must be carefully "chunked"—broken up into inviting bits of written and visual content to be easily consumed. Finally, these channels are for organizations that really have something to say and can back it up with data, illustrations, and so on. That's why these channels tend to be more popular, at least for now, with B2B marketers, although digital magazines will doubtless open long-form content up to B2C marketers in the near future.

Figure 10.14   *Eloqua's Grande Guides to marketing with social media contained well-organized, bite-sized chunks of how-to information that attract measurable business results to the company*

User Base:

As discussed, long-form content is for organizations with plenty of intellectual capital that have conducted original research or that offer complex products and services.

Digital Media Center/Press Room

Description:

An online press or media center is an area of a website devoted to the needs of the media. It's important to bear in mind that although media should be considered the primary audience, they'll hardly be the only one (see "User Base"). Given that close to 100% of working journalists research companies and executives they cover online, this is the ground zero area of your site to serve the media. Content includes media contact information (phone numbers and email addresses), archived press releases, downloadable press kits, executive bios and headshots, backgrounders and fact sheets, events and timelines, awards and recognitions, an "in the news" section of recent media citations, company history, and opportunities to subscribe to RSS feeds of company news and to opt in to the organization's media email list.

Heifer International, a global charity, offers an excellent online press room. (Though "media" room is a far more appropriate name for it these days.) Contact information is front and center, so are opportunities to subscribe to news and easily access multimedia digital assets so journalists can embellish stories with images and video (see Figure 10.15).

Figure 10.15   *Have a cow! Heifer International wants you, and for a good cause. They make it easy for journalists and others to spread its message in its online press room.*

Pros:

Few organizations don't seek media coverage. The purpose of a communications or public relations division is to make journalist queries, research, and requests for information easy and accessible. A digital media center serves exactly that purpose, with the added advantage of accessibility to the public, investors, or others seeking that same information. Transparency and easy access to information are in high demand and foundational to any marketing effort. That should be both the purpose and the goal of any online media center.

Designing an online media center with SEO principles in mind will also help ensure that those researching an organization via search engines will have a better chance of finding information straight from the source. Options such as mailing lists and really simple syndication (RSS) feeds can help you stay in touch and engaged with those tracking you or your industry.

The American Cancer Society understands the value of not waiting for visitors to their media pages, but making a variety of feeds available to interested users (see Figure 10.16).

Figure 10.16   *A variety of different RSS feeds targeted to different audiences is smart strategy. Consider feeds for breaking news, corporate announcements, investor relations, and regional divisions of a company or organization.*

Cons:

In addition to committing time and resources into building an online media center, such an initiative obviously requires ongoing maintenance and updating.

User Base:

As mentioned already, an online media center is primarily for the media: members of the working press, broadcast journalists, and of course, increasingly bloggers and others who track and report company or industry news and information. Given that most organizations with a media center include them as part of their overall website (or corporate site), the content is publicly accessible and available to anyone.

Apps and Widgets

Description:

There's overlap between apps and widgets. So for our purposes here, let's define apps as mobile applications for smartphones (for example, iPhones, Androids, or Blackberrys) or tablets that allow users to perform specific tasks or access specific information. Widgets do much the same thing but tend to be embedded into websites rather than mobile-accessible platforms. There are, for example, many Facebook applications that would fall into this definition of "widget." Apple has made recent strides to incorporate widgets into computer operating systems, promising even more ubiquity in the foreseeable future.

Pros:

For brands with a high degree of user loyalty and engagement (think nutrition or fitness, for example) or time-sensitive information (publishers, news organizations), apps and widgets can extend that loyalty into everyday life. Because most apps and widgets are custom built and quite literally portable, they extend awareness and utility into users' everyday lives.

Because widgets are largely accessed on mobile platforms, many incorporate functionality related to information a user needs— now! Of course, what you need now can vary widely, as shown in Figure 10.17. Kraft want to help you decide what to make for dinner tonight and will deliver a shopping list to your phone. As you can see in Figure 10.18, Charmin addresses an even more urgent need: Where's the nearest potty (and how clean is it)? Finally, as you can see in Figure 10.19, HSBC want to be there for you when you need to check your bank balance, find the nearest ATM, or contact a rep.

> "Because most apps and widgets are custom built and quite literally portable, they extend awareness and utility into users' everyday lives."

Figure 10.17 *What's for dinner, and what do you need to buy to make it? Kraft puts ideas, and shopping lists, literally at your fingertips*

Figure 10.18 *When you gotta go, you gotta go. Charmin wants to point you in the right direction.*

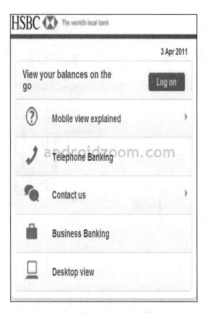

Figure 10.19   *Find a local branch, check your balance, speak with a rep. HSBC's widget puts the bank in your pocket.*

Many apps function like mini, customized search engines, helping shoppers buy food or search recipes (Kraft), find a nearby restroom that's clean (Charmin's SitorSquat), or locate your banks' nearest ATM (HSBC). Publishers such as the New York Times and ESPN (see Figure 10.20) deliver news, headlines, and sport scores.

Figure 10.20   *The New York Times app offers news, headlines, and sports scores.*

Apps and widgets can also encourage interaction. Numerous Facebook apps contain quiz or polling features, as well as games, and publish results or scores to the player's Facebook page, publicizing the feature to that person's social network.

Cons:

You need to get this right the first time. Particularly on mobile platforms, if an app doesn't work out of the box, it will be abandoned. Obviously, usage of apps and widgets is higher among younger and more technically sophisticated audiences. B2B organizations are getting to the game a little later, but with some creativity they can build opportunities. GE, for example, built GE Transformers, a mobile app that monitors the health of transformer equipment in the field (as shown in Figure 10.21). It offers powerful custom graphing tools and interactive mapping of transformer locations.

User Base:

Apps and widgets should not only be easy to use, but also have a compelling reason for people to use them regularly—daily or weekly, or to accomplish tasks or glean information they frequently need.

Figure 10.21   *GE Transformers is a mobile app that monitors the health of transformer equipment in the field.*

Case Studies

Description:

A case study is a document of how your organization successfully accomplished a client engagement or account to the benefit of that party. It's a short-form (a page or two) account in narrative form, often accompanied by graphics, testimonials, or charts, that clearly outlines the advantages provided to the client. Some companies feature case studies in video format on their sites. The format of a typical case study is to first state the Business Challenge, move on to the Approach or Solution used to solve or address it, then discuss Results.

Pros:

Case studies build credibility and trust. They illustrate and demonstrate that you can successfully provide the services and benefits you claim, with the bonus that they're endorsed by a third-party: the client.

Cons:

In many industries, it can be difficult or nearly impossible to get clients' permission to use their name in a case study. Newer businesses without a track record and client roster face formidable challenges.

User Base:

Case studies are most often used in service industries rather than by companies that sell products.

Articles and Columns

Description:

Like speaking at industry events, bylined articles and columns get names and thought-leadership "out there" when organizations' executives contribute to external publications.

Pros:

Articles highlight thought-leadership, observations on industry trends, and innovation in an excellent forum: objective, third-party publications under editorial guidance.

Cons:

Writing for publications means following their editorial guidelines and above all, not being pitch-y or sales-y. One-hit wonders rarely do the job, so consider pitching a series of articles, articles seeding to numerous publications, or a regular column. When editing a leading business publication, one of my regular contributors swore it took, on average for contributors, nine months before benefits such as invitations to speak at conferences and new business inquiries were forthcoming. Like branding campaigns, article publishing must be ongoing to be effective.

User Base:

Bylined contributions to publications are particularly valuable for consultants and firms who offer consulting or professional services or any arena in which it's important to demonstrate depth and breadth of knowledge, trends, or new technologies.

Elearning/Online Training

Many products and services are complex to use; sophisticated software applications are just one example of highly specialized products with a steep, steep learning curve. That's where elearning or digital training comes in. It can take many forms: self-directed online courses (many commercial elearning software packages are on the market), videos, podcasts, and webinars being the prime examples. Salesforce.com is an outstanding example. The company offers a robust and highly customizable digital customer relationship management solution that's widely used in a number of industries. Together with the actual product, Salesforce has developed training and certification courses—88 of them at present time—targeted at different cohorts of their core customer base: end users, administrators, developers, consultants. Courses can be delivered in person, on-demand, or in "virtual classrooms," Salesforce.com's very extensive training offerings are shown in Figures 10.22 and 10.23.

Companies such as IBM and SAP have created online communities for their clients that are in part targeted at training. In these forums, customers help other customers in peer discussions.

Pros:

Clearly, the first and foremost benefit of training is helping customers use a company's product to its full advantage, and in a way that's tailored to their specific needs. Digital training can also significantly reduce customer service costs. A well-monitored training program can also become a feedback loop that aids product development as trainers or data reveals where customers are experiencing problems. Finally, this post-sales customer touchpoint can help up- or cross-sell additional products or services.

Figure 10.22   *Digital CRM solutions provider Salesforce.com has sliced and diced its offering so they're findable for job role, format or product.*

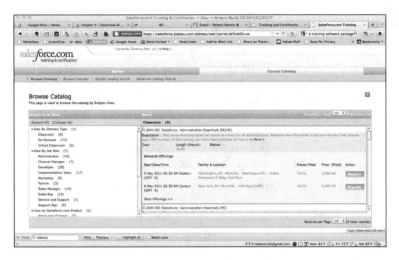

Figure 10.23 *Training can be a critical component in selling complex software solutions, such as Salesforce.com's tools. Who better to teach users how to use it than the company behind the product?*

Cons:

Online training is obviously not for products that are simple to use. An enterprise software package, yes. A toothbrush? Not so much. And although online training can greatly help reduce customer support costs, it will not completely eliminate the need for support.

User Base:

Complex and specialized offerings, particularly in software, technology, and engineering, make up the user base. It's less for consumer goods than for B2B organizations.

Online Community

Description:

A community is a microsite that's part of a larger organization's or brand's web presence. Communities come in two flavors: company-focused and user/consumer focused. An example of the former is Microsoft's Channel 9, an ongoing collection of videos of "the people behind the products." In "The Channel 9 Doctrine," the company states explicitly that, "Channel 9 is not a marketing tool, not a PR tool, not a lead generation tool," but rather a place where the company can "learn by listening." Although the site is primarily video-focused, it also features blogs, a feedback forum, a Twitter presence, and more (see Figure 10.24).

Figure 10.24   *Microsoft's Channel 9.*

Consumer-focused community sites invite participation from the outside: from buyers, users, prospects, and enthusiasts. Autotrader, for example, has a community for that subset of its clientele that's enthusiastic about classic and vintage cars (see Figure 10.25). Members can share tips, advice, and opinions, take polls, and post photos of their rides. In a sense, it's a social network for classic car enthusiasts.

Figure 10.25   *An Autotrader community dedicated to classic and vintage car enthusiasts.*

Similiarly, there are community sites for moms (J&J's BabyCenter.com is a prime example), for software service and support ranging from Apple's user support communities that number in the hundreds—for every model of hardware and software the company has ever issued, to similar communities for enterprise-level software such as IBM or SAP.

Pros:

Communities are great for organizations that can engage passionate audiences around areas of their interest. Books, politics, travel, technology, and health and wellness are all prime example. If you sell milk or some other sort of commoditized good, you're probably not a candidate for launching a community. Communities can leverage fans into spokespersons and create enormous goodwill. They can help create and sustain a transparent and accessible brand personality while assuring customers that they're central to organizational success and their needs are not only listened to, but addressed. A community's most loyal and prolific participants can be rewarded or tasked with administrative duties, relieving the sponsoring organization of at least some of the work involved in maintaining and monitoring the community.

Cons:

A community is no place to sell. As stated previously, it's not for commodities or products and services about which customers aren't somewhat passionate. Most of the solid consumer-oriented topics are already "taken," which means extra thought and creativity will have to be invested into newer communities to really attract a loyal user base.

User Base:

Brands, products, or services around which there's passion, dedication, and engagement make up the user base. This might include brands with an enormous fan base (Apple); popular activities in which people are deeply involved (baby and child care, pets, autos, cooking, and recipes); health and wellness (dieting, vegetarianism, exercise), or more complex B2B issues, such as using complex technology offerings.

Wikis

Description:

Wikipedia is a wiki, though you're likely more familiar with the collaborative online encyclopedia than with the term "wiki." Fundamentally, a wiki is a collaboration platform that allows visitors (generally, registered visitors) to add, create, and edit content on a specific topic or area of knowledge. NetConcepts, for example, an SEO company, created a wiki to define common search terms (see Figure 10.26).

Figure 10.26   *The NetConcepts Wiki defines common search terms.*

Pros:

Wikis are primarily used internally by collaborative teams, often separated by geography and time differences. But for highly complex products and services (think engineering, soft- and hardware, industrial supplies), wikis can be invaluable for creating a base of knowledge. They're also a great way to attract passionate and committed thinkers and experts eager to share their opinions.

Cons:

Because wikis are at their core collaborative, expect disagreements (sometimes fighting and arguments), and forget the notion of staying in control.

User Base:

In this case, the user base is composed of companies comfortable with handing over the reins and that have the patience to slowly develop a presence. Rome wasn't built in a day. It will take time to attract the right users and induce them to contribute to and help build a useful and substantive wiki.

Visual Information (Charts, Diagrams, Infographics, Maps)

Description:

Pictures, images and graphics capture attention and interest. That's why graphic images (independent of photos and videos) are a critical part of a content marketing arsenal (see Figure 10.27). Think complex information portrayed graphically in the form of charts, diagrams, infographics, and other forms of graphic visualization.

Figure 10.27   *Images are an integral part of a successful content marketing arsenal.*

Pros:

Images make complex, hard-to-digest material immediately graspable and under-standable. They can tell stories, and above all, they translate abstract numerical data into concepts people can readily grasp. Images and graphics are also shareable and help in the dissemination of storytelling. Often, images can stand on their own to tell as story, while of course being an invaluable resource as an accompaniment to articles, research reports, press releases, and news stories.

Cons:

Aside from committing resources to creating a standard for clear and attractive graphic imaging, there are virtually no drawbacks to the relevant and intelligent use of imagery.

User Base:

Any company telling stories or conveying information that's rich in data, numbers, or statistics makes up the user base. Complex relationships are often better expressed visually (think organizational or flow chart) than using mere words.

11

Content and SEO

"Nothing matters more in search engine optimization than content. Nothing."

Sure, technical aspects of a site play a large factor, as does site architecture. A few things done improperly or mismanaged (for example, a robots.txt file, a line of code that prevents a search engine from even seeing online content) can torpedo search engine optimization (SEO) efforts. But when it comes to having a well-optimized web presence that's visible to search engines, content is the alpha and omega of those efforts. More specifically, written content matters. Search engines can only crawl, index, and understand text—not images, videos, podcasts, photos, or any other type of graphic or multimedia content.

That's not to say you can't optimize nontext content marketing elements. We'll examine how later in this chapter.

Keywords Are Key

Strong, optimized written copy is the most critical part of any SEO initiative. However, before the first sentence, tagline, or headline is written, be sure to identify those keywords and key phrases your target audience is likely to use when searching for your website, articles, blog entries, or other content initiatives. Also, make sure you do the same for individual pages or specific pieces of content within a website or blog.

These are the words and phrases *searchers* use, not necessarily the ones you use back at the office when you're talking with colleagues. Perhaps you're a medical professional who bandies about terms such as "myocardial infraction." The average Web searcher is more likely to seek information on "heart attack."

The first step in the keyword research process is simply to brainstorm a list of the words and phrases a searcher might use to find your site or business. The trick here is to be specific. Forget broad terms like "shoes." Focus instead on "running shoes" or "wedding shoes" or "Nike running shoes" or "black patent leather high-heeled pumps." It can be helpful to ask outsiders such as friends, family, clients, or colleagues what terms come to mind.

After the initial list is in hand, the next step is to determine how useful these terms really are. That's where keyword research tools come in handy.

> ✉ *Note*
>
> Both Google and Bing offer free keyword research tools. They require you to first sign up for an advertiser account, but no worries—they don't compel you to run ads to use the free tools.

By running the list of proposed keywords through a keyword research tool, you'll learn how many searchers are actually conducting searches for a given word or term every day, how many of those searches actually converted into sales or another desired action (that is, a whitepaper download), and other analytical information. These tools can also make you aware of words not on the list, or synonyms.

This information should narrow down the selections to a final list of keywords. Plug these into a spreadsheet that helps you visualize at a glance each word or phrase's conversion rate, search volume, and competition. This list helps narrow your focus and concentrates on the most important terms for your content. Don't completely eliminate broad terms such as "shoes" because these give searchers a general feel for what you're offering. However, it's the specific, targeted terms ("pink suede ballerina flats") that attract the targeted traffic at the bottom of the purchase or conversion funnel.

The best keywords have certain characteristics:

- **Strong relevance**—Terms for which you have content to support.

- **Relatively high search volume**—Terms people actually search for.

- **Relatively low competition**—Terms with a small number of search results, that is other pages on the Internet that search engines have indexed as containing a specific word or phrase.

After you've determined which keywords to target—both for an overall content marketing initiative as well as for specific, smaller campaigns—it's time to build content around those terms. Bear in mind that search engines reward high-quality, original content more than virtually anything else out there. This is why content aggregation is fine (and relevant), but also why aggregation should almost always be regularly supplemented with well-written and researched original content.

A major way that search engine algorithms to determine quality content is by examining how many links there are to specific pieces of content. Links can almost be considered "votes" vouching for quality content. As far as search engines are concerned, this isn't the most democratic process in the world; a link from a major metropolitan daily such as *The New York Times* is a higher-ranking vote than one from, say, a random tweet on Twitter. And a link from a site that is semantically similar obviously make more sense—and therefore counts more—than a link from something willy-nilly, say a site about politics linking to a page about Christmas cookie recipes.

One of the best strategies for getting people to link to you is, of course, to link to them. Another approach is to follow relevant sites, blogs, online video channels, and social networking presences in your particular vertical and to comment on them, with appropriate and relevant links back to your own content. Authoring articles and other types of content for third-party sites is also a valuable link strategy; most of these have an "about the author" blurb that creates a link back to your own site or blog. Internal links are also highly valuable because links are what search engine spiders follow to find content in the first place. This is where site maps, tags, category pages, and well-considered taxonomies come in handy. They not only help visitors find relevant content, they help search engines find it, too.

Making content as sharable as possible is another valuable link-building strategy. It's why so many sites contain those small icons encouraging visitors to "share on Facebook or LinkedIn or Digg or Delicious," or "Tweet this." Individually, social media links might not be as valuable as that *New York Times* citation, but many sites are seeing highly significant portions of their traffic originating from social media sites thanks to such efforts.

To this end, content authors should also be regarded as important link-building sources, particularly guest or third-party content contributors who can leverage links through their own websites or social networks to build links that benefit both parties.

Crispin Sheridan, the senior director of search marketing at global software giant SAP, led an initiative to integrate the company's social media presence with SEO that resulted in conversion rate increasing 250% (see Figure 11.1).

"We did a kind of a mini-audit and looked at how many social media sites that seemed to be about SAP were out there. That's when we discovered the large number of blogs—well, we already knew about the blogs," said Sheridan. "I think the 22-plus active Twitter accounts came as a surprise, the 17-plus Facebook fan pages, the various LinkedIn groups, a lot of content on YouTube, but none of it really coming from official channels. So we realized there was a lot of activity going on."

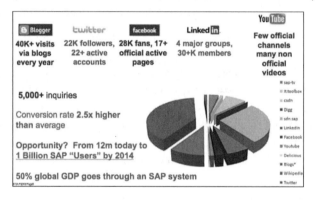

Figure 11.1   *When SAP conducted an audit of the brand's unofficial social media presence, the results astounded the internal team. The company wasn't producing a great deal of content, but users were.*

Sheridan's team began using the keywords present in all those external social media sites—the words and phrases people interested in the company were using when they talked about the company and its products and services. The question posed: "If we use those same keywords in social media activities such as Facebook fans pages, wall posts, links—what kinds of traffic would we see, and would it be valuable traffic?"

The company built a Facebook fan page up to a statistically relevant sample size for the organization. (Its target was 16,000 fans but now exceeds 25,000.) By using the top value and highest converting keywords and phrases from its organic search efforts, it began creating posts for the Facebook page with those same terms.

"That's when we realized the traffic that was coming in [through social media channels] was converting at 2.5 times the amount of organic search traffic," Sheridan says.

"We believe the high conversion rate is because these people are very much engaged; they're the ones we call the e-fluentials. They're the ones who are beginning to reach out to their peers and consult other people, which usually means they're farther down in the buying cycle than the people who are kicking the tires. Maybe they don't want to talk with a salesperson yet, be bothered, or even divulge that they're looking, but we found that the people coming to us seem to be at a lower stage in the funnel: the buying process."

This is a stunning example of applying SEO principles to social media and other content channels, not to mention a solid reason for having keyword research in place.

Optimize Images and Multimedia Content

As stated in the opening of this chapter, search engines can't read anything other than plain old text. They can't watch a video, listen to an audio file, or assign a thousand words to a picture. So to optimize images and multimedia content for search, you have to create the words for the search engines.

What all these file types have in common is a need for clear, descriptive names or titles. These are not by any means the default name spit out by audio, video, or image software, such as img230769.jpg. Filenames should be as descriptive as possible and match what the file represents.

If you have a shot of an apple, for example, call it a "New York State Macintosh Apple," or "Ripe Harvest Orchard's Macoun Apple," not just plain old "apple." For all a search engine knows, that "apple" could be a computer or even a mobile phone.

Such descriptive names not only are found by search engine spiders, they often have the added advantage of appearing above, below, or by the image itself, enhancing the user experience as well. Beyond any other optimization tactics, filenames are accorded the most weight by search engines when it comes to ranking.

It should, therefore, come as no surprise that websites that regularly use multiple media files require a naming strategy or protocol to ensure consistency in the names used for graphics, audio, or video.

After giving media files clear, descriptive names, don't forget to add more descriptive text (or meta data) to the "alt" attribute in the file's tag. Make it short and to the point, like the filename. This is an opportunity to go a little bit broader. That New York State apple, for example, might be from Olsen's Orchards or have been a product of the 2011 harvest, or perhaps this is the place to indicate it's a sweet, crisp, delicious, and nutritious apple.

Online merchants might want to use this field to add information such as a manufacturer, product category, or UPC code.

Let's say you sell DVDs online. The name of the media file, in this case a photo of the cover art, would obviously be the title of the film. The "alt" attribute might include the names of the actors, director, studio, genre, release year, and any miscellaneous information such as "Academy Award Nominee."

Perhaps the media file in question is named "Lady Gaga on American Idol." The meta data might refer to the specific contestant in the competition or the names of other judges, or it might list some of the singer's credits, so the video shows up on more general searches by her fans.

Keyword strategy, combined with content marketing goals, will inform what type of additional data is added in this section.

A caption adjacent to an image or media file helps search engines "understand" what the file is about because adjacent text helps search engines contextualize what they've found and determine relevancy. The goal here is to function much like a newspaper or a magazine by adding keyword-rich captions to files. This way, even if someone's been careless and named an image file Bass.jpg, the adjacent text and caption can help a search engine understand if the image depicts a fish, a musical instrument, or a particular brand of shoe. This approach can be broadened to optimizing the entire page the media file resides on to further increase the depth of context and relevancy.

In the case of images, file type matters. Photos should be rendered in .jpg format, and logos should be .gif files. The reason is simply that these are standard formats that search engines "expect" to find. Search engines assume a .gif file has 256 colors, which is standard for rendering graphics such as logos, whereas photos are rendered in millions of colors. And when using logo files, it's all-important that the file be named with whatever's in that logo. No search engine is smart enough to deduce that a simple .gif file represents the logo for Bank of America, Ikea, or Acme Exterminating.

Although it can be labor-intensive, posting a Hypertext Markup Language (HTML) transcript of the dialogue in an audio or video file goes extraordinarily far in terms of optimizing the actual content of these media files. Given the nature of the medium, it's best to keep these files short—optimally five minutes or less (particularly in the case of video). Cutting longer media files into shorter segments not only eases viewing, but also affords additional opportunities to optimize the content and to provide extra, spider-able links between episodes or installments. This is particularly helpful in the case of episodic videos or podcasts.

Quality Matters—So Does Specificity

It's not just content that reigns supreme in SEO; it's *quality* content. Google's own published guidelines on the topic say in essence that all those hoping to rank well in search should write for their own visitors and users, not for the search engines themselves. The company is putting its algorithms solidly behind this recommendation. In recent years, we've seen content farms, which are websites that churn out mountains of garbage content to game the search engines and rise to the top of organic search results, plummet, and in many cases even disappear from search rankings.

> "It's not just content that reigns supreme in SEO; it's *quality* content."

Creating a lot of garbage is, of course, cheap and easy. Creating—and sustaining the creation of—high-quality content requires thought and investment (particularly when everyone else is trying to do it, too).

There are plenty of good reasons to keep content interesting, informative, entertaining, engaging, witty, useful, well written and well presented. Dozens of reasons to have a strong taxonomy, descriptive and compelling headlines, tags, and other organizational attributes. Now you can add SEO to that list, too. You may be creating and publishing the best content on the Web—but what does that matter if no one can find it?

12

Content and PR

Public relations (PR) just plain doesn't work the way it used to.

In a way, PR is one of the original forms of content marketing. PRs do plenty of things, of course: publicity, reputation management, and media relations, to name but a few. But the heart and sole of PR has always been planting stories in the media: in newspapers, magazine, television, and radio. With the exception of "the exclusive," the primary tool in the arsenal for planting stories has been the press release—a brief, persuasive, one- or two-page document intended to persuade its journalist recipients that the topic was worth their time, attention, and coverage.

Press releases don't work that way anymore because they're no longer a private, one-to-one communications channel. (Once upon a time, releases were mailed, and later faxed, to newsrooms.) In an age of press releases distributed over wire services—wire services that are immediately picked up by all the major news services including Google, Yahoo, AOL News, and Bing—the second a press release is released, the PR practitioner has already broken his own story. It's hard to persuade people in the news business to pick up "news" once the story is already "out there."

So although PR practitioners were once exclusively in the business of influencing the media (and they still are), they (like all other content marketers) are themselves the media. Moreover, they interface and target a media landscape that's grown far beyond traditional press and broadcasts outlets.

That's a real game changer.

Yet fundamentals remain the same. PRs are good at shaping and spreading stories, and content marketing is, as we've seen, very much about stories. In a digital landscape, this necessitates not only finding and shaping stories, but also determining how they are told, through which channels, and to whom.

Enter the Optimized Press Release

The press release isn't dead in the context of content marketing. Instead, it's optimized for a variety of different target audiences as well as for search engines. Given that after a release crosses the wire it's "out there" for anyone to find (not just journalists), keyword research has become an essential component of optimizing the press release for search. When the two or three relevant search terms the target audience is most likely to search for are determined, they are incorporated into the headline and opening paragraph of the release. It's become increasingly important that press releases contain links: to video, photos, executive bios, a company or product website—anything that will expand upon the story.

SEO-PR, a company specializing in this approach, experimented in 2010 with optimized and unoptimized versions of the same press release from Rutgers University (see Figure 12.1). It announced that the students enrolling in the university's mini-MBA program in digital marketing would receive an iPad containing essential course materials for the program. A YouTube video on the iPad's role in the program was also developed.

> "The press release isn't dead in the context of content marketing."

The unoptimized press release was headlined "Rutgers to Put iPad to the Test in New Digital Marketing Program," with virtually no pick-up (other than by a publication with which one of the partners of the PR firms had a business relationship). Six days later, the optimized release went out with the headline "Apple iPad Tablet to Be Tested in New Rutgers Mini-MBA Digital Marketing Executive Education Courses." This longer headline includes additional search terms: Apple iPad, Apple iPad tablet, mini-MBA, Rutgers mini-MBA, executive education, and executive education courses.

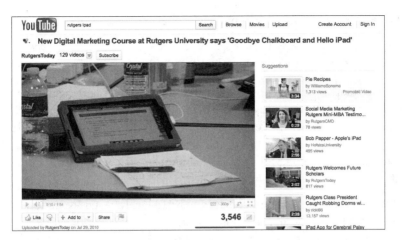

Figure 12.1   *Note the keywords in the headline of this optimized press release.*

According to Business Wire's NewsTrak Access Report, the optimized press release received 22,027 headline impressions, 819 release views, and 35 link clicks. Page views on the Rutgers University landing page for the program not only rose 116% percent, but also generated the first registrations for the program.

In other words, it was a highly successful press release, but not necessarily one aimed at the press.

Find the Influencers (Not Necessarily the Journalists)

The example in the previous section illustrates that end users, potential buyers, students, and clients can be the target of the press release, whereas in bygone days that target was limited to the press. At one time, PRs jealously maintained, guarded, and updated media lists—their who's-covering-what-beat Rolodex of who to reach out to when placing stories. However, now their challenge is to target influencers with PR. Influencers can be bloggers or others with a significant social media following who are talking online about the issues or products or services that fit with whatever a PR is working to publicize. And, unlike the mainstream media, these essential targets are not necessarily versed or experienced in dealing with PR professionals.

This lays out a new set of challenges:

- Identifying the influencers
- Building relationships with them

- Finding the online communities where relevant discussions occur

- Creating awareness and enough enthusiasm to encourage these people and groups to discuss the product/service/story

FLOR, a company specializing in carpeting and other interior design products, engaged Meritus Media's Sally Falkow to bring the story of the launch of a modular carpet line by designer Alexander Girard to relevant online communities. Falkow broke down the target audiences as follows: top bloggers in design and home decorating; hip young urban professionals; and mothers with an interest in do-it-yourself (DIY) design. Before delivering content, listening was critical.

"Much of the blogging success comes from being involved and seeing opportunities," said Falkow, "Social media is not as cut and dried as traditional PR is. We had to constantly read and monitor blogs to see where there was an opportunity to comment or refer readers to content that was generated."

In addition to generating influence, Falkow was able to persuade several influential bloggers to run a contest to win a free rug. One particularly influential blog drew more than 500 entries. Apartment Therapy, a blog with 1.5 million monthly visitors, mentioned the product four times. All in all, more than 200 bloggers responded with interest to the story. But bear in mind this wasn't about creating a release and sending it out, but rather following and participating in conversations over time, so the content would be relevant to the target audience, as well as presented appropriately and in context.

Joining conversations and then supplying appropriate content is only one approach to PR content marketing initiatives. Another is a more classic approach rooted firmly in predigital PR: creating a story and talking points around the product being publicized. Another example from Sally Falkow is a campaign created for HerRoom.com, a site that sells intimate apparel (see Figure 12.2).

The challenge was to sell the company's line of sports bras and to draw attention to the videos explaining the benefits of each model. For each of the 25 or so different sports bras sold on the site, a video had been produced to highlight the actual performance of the garment in action: Shoppers could watch a woman's torso jogging in the bra. To complement this content offering and attract attention to the videos, the site also featured a podcast by an expert, Dr. Joanna Scurr of the UK's Portsmouth University, on her research into the dynamics of breast movement, the risks of breast damage from vigorous physical activity, and what sports bras work best.

Figure 12.2   *Every product has its own informative, illustrative video. And a podcast narrated by an academic subject-matter expert further helps women to make the right choice when selecting a sports bra.*

The videos were posted, but hardly viewed. The podcast by a medical expert was added, both to optimize the content and to present it in a more interesting contextual fashion. It worked.

A SEO-optimized press released garnered significant coverage of Scurr's findings, including a *New York Times* article. Several years after the campaign launched, HerRoom.com still ranks number one for "sports bra test" and "bounce test" on Google.

A major takeaway from the above case studies should be the importance of PR practitioners asking themselves, "Who's the audience?" Sure, it can be journalists. But it can also be the general public and influencers in a given field, whether bloggers, online discussion groups, or people with a significant number of Twitter followers who stick to a specific topic of coverage. These latter groups are not accustomed to dealing with PR people, but they are open and receptive to discussing their passions with interested, receptive, and informed contributors to the conversation.

In addition to joining conversations, it's critical in a world of content that it be easy to talk about—and to share. Chapter 10 discussed the importance of creating a robust online media center for media or anyone else needing to know more about an organization. At the very least it should be a well-organized repository for news, press mentions, media contacts, press releases, investor information (in the case of public companies), executive photos and bios, product shots, and an online video archive with embed codes so media can easily be shared and disseminated. Press kits should be available, and they should be multimedia.

"Forward-thinking companies are beginning to take the online newsroom a step further. They're creating social newsrooms."

Forward-thinking companies are beginning to take the online newsroom a step further. They're creating social newsrooms. Chemical company BASF not only frequently updates the content on its social media newsroom—in multiple languages—but invites the media and others interested in the company to follow it on Twitter, Facebook, YouTube, Slideshare, and Flickr (see Figure 12.3).

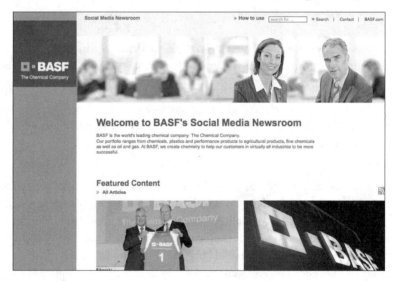

Figure 12.3   *BASF's social media newsroom features widgets that display the latest content uploaded to platforms such as Facebook, Flickr, Twitter, YouTube, and Slideshare.*

Content is content, and BASF understands it can both disseminate and aggregate company-related content at the same time—while making it easy for others to do the same. Effectively, the social media newsroom is a hub for all the company's social media (read: content) activities.

The Winston-Salem Convention and Visitors Bureau has a social media newsroom that it made available to all members—hotels, restaurants, sports venues, museums, and so on—so they could update news themselves using the PRESSfeed newsroom platform (see Figure 12.4).

It's an ingenious solution for an organization that's a consortium of dozens of businesses, and one that's resulted in marked traffic increases for the participants. The page also makes it easy for journalists and other subscribers to access the information of interest to them via RSS feeds covering different aspects of the region: conventions, enriching experiences, and local sporting events.

It's also giving the target audience what they want—and need. A Web Influencers study from 2010 indicates that journalists are asking for more video and images with news release. They also want to embed codes with digital assets to easily incorporate them into web-based coverage. Yet in the U.S., only 11% of corporate newsrooms offer these features.

Figure 12.4 *The PRESSfeed newsroom platform in action.*

13

Content and Advertising

"In digital environments, it's as easy to become media as it is to buy media."

Content and advertising have always been either/or propositions in the context of traditional print and broadcast media. Advertising (or commercials) existed in a clearly circumscribed periphery outside, or adjacent to, the main content that was created by the publisher or broadcaster. Advertising was interruptive. It was the price that readers or viewers paid to get free or subsidized content. Those lines blurred slightly (but only slightly) in certain contexts, such as "advertorial" sections in magazines.

Advertising—in which an advertiser buys the media in which they place a commercial message—is still distinct from editorial content, or programming, but the lines are blurring in the digital environment. You need only look at "traditional" publishers including Gannett, Meredith, Hearst, and most recently Condé Nast, that are buying up digital technology and digital agencies (or, in some cases, establishing their own in-house) to help their advertisers reach deeper into digital marketing with content, apps, social media programs, ecommerce offerings, and the like.

Condé Nast Ideactive, for example, is an in-house agency that specifically goes after the *nonmedia* budgets of Condé Nast's advertising clients. Lou Cona, who heads the venture, said when it launched in May 2011, "We can tap into our experts if people want custom content. This is not about repurposing, although some of it could be. If someone wants custom content related to fashion and beauty, for example, we have the consumer insights to develop it."

In other words, experts in content creation such as the firms that publish periodicals ranging from *Vogue* to *The New Yorker* are helping brands not only to correctly situate their ads, but also create compelling *content* that will appeal to those magazines' audiences.

Content is what advertisers are demanding. In digital environments, it's as easy to *become* media as it is to *buy* media. Advertising, advertorial, content…the lines are blurring in ways that defy precise definitions.

A quasi-advertorial example might be the campaign Coke Light undertook in France in 2010, partnering both with fashion designer Karl Lagerfeld and with Yahoo France. In the past the beverage company had asked fashion designers to redesign the Coke Light bottle. With Lagerfeld's bottle, it went further.

Lagerfeld agreed to design a bottle featuring his immediately recognizable silhouette. He also designed the ads for the new packaging himself (see Figures 13.1 and 13.2).

Figure 13.1   *Karl Lagerfeld's recognizable silhouette graced these bottles.*

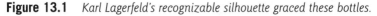

Coke decided that it needed its own content platform for all this material to "live" in, so it partnered with Yahoo France to create a content platform. This platform became a dedicated online fashion channel, The Daily Woman, targeting women aged 25 to 39. The site's production values are as high as anything you'd expect from a "real" online fashion magazine. At launch, all content was surrounded by Coke Light skins reflecting the Lagerfeld aesthetic.

Advertising? Advertorial? Branded Entertainment? Tough to say, exactly—but it's certainly a form of content marketing.

Figure 13.2   *Coke partnered with Karl Lagerfeld to create this ad.*

Many major brands are using advertising to drive target audiences into deeper brand experiences through immersive content. Earlier, we looked at examples such as the American Express Seinfeld-Superman campaign, or the Microsoft teaming of the same comedian with its then-CEO Bill Gates. Both campaigns were notable for media buys that drove viewers online for more content-rich messaging.

Another example is Dove's Calming Night campaign (see Figure 13.3). Targeted at moms, the campaign goal was to get women to change their skincare regimen and begin taking a shower at night rather than in the hectic morning.

Figure 13.3   *Dove's Calming Night campaign.*

Print ads in entertainment magazines and TV commercials on NBC and ABC encouraged women to go online to tune into the "real" campaign: webisodes, or online mini-movies. In each, the leading character uses the Calming Night product following a stressful parenting situation, which results in a revitalizing sleep and pleasant dreams.

Mothers watched more than 46,000 hours of Dove's webisodes, with more than five million page views of all the content and sponsored areas. One million product samples were requested and delivered.

The Dove webisodes were directed by Penny Marshall and featured Hollywood talent, a tactic also adopted by BMW in one of the first successful online webisode campaigns, "The Hire." The company engaged eight top directors—John Frankenheimer,

Ang Lee, Wong Kar-wai, Guy Ritchie, Alejandro González Iñárritu, John Woo, Joe Carnahan, and Tony Scott—who each directed a 10-minute film featuring a BMW being put through its moves in a loose narrative scenario. The series proved so popular that a DVD was issued (see Figure 13.4). During the first year of the campaign, BMW rose 12% over the previous year. The movies were viewed more than 11 million times in four months. Two million people registered with the website, and a majority of users who had registered on the site sent film links to friends and family.

Figure 13.4   *BMW's "The Hire."*

Another successful example of webisodes is "Easy to Assemble," Ikea's series featuring actress Illeana Douglas as a fictionalized version of herself who quits acting and gets a job at the store (see Figure 13.5).

Figure 13.5   *IKEA Easy to Assemble ads.*

Yet another content marketing tactic strongly linked with content marketing is telling the "making of" backstory of the production of a commercial spot, particularly one that's popular or technically sophisticated. Old Spice had an extraordinarily successful campaign, "The Man Your Man Could Smell Like." YouTube featured the spots, but these "making of" short films garnered up to a million views on the channel, as well as mentions in blogs and news stories (see Figure 13.6). Toyota did much the same thing with making-of videos for its Prius Harmony spot, as had shoemaker Adidas (see Figure 13.7).

Figure 13.6   *Old Spice's extremely successful "The Man Your Man Could Smell Like" campaign.*

Figure 13.7   *Adidas "Making the Commercial."*

Advertising actually becomes content on YouTube and other online video destinations. Brands that invest millions of dollars in Super Bowl campaigns can attract millions of additional viewers—at no additional media buying cost—by making those spots available for tune-in whenever viewers want to revisit the ads. And revisit they do. Not only Super Bowl ads, but also other cool ads such as Sony Bravia's bouncing balls (see Figure 13.8) or Blendtec's "Will It Blend" campaign have garnered millions and millions of extra views online—at zero extra media spend.

Figure 13.8   *Sony Bravia Ad.*

Video isn't, of course, the only way to link up advertising with content marketing. A stunning recent example of a really great story, coupled with a really minimal media buy, comes for the Centers for Disease Control and Prevention (CDC). Federal agencies are rarely accorded lavish media budgets, but a healthy dose of creativity and imagination got the CDC's message about emergency preparedness across in a big, big way.

The value proposition: how to survive a zombie apocalypse.

The "ads" for the campaign were nothing more than small units users could add to their websites, Facebook pages, and so on. Ads indeed, but zero media cost. Content told the story, and a blog post got it "out there."

In May 2011, author Ali S. Khan asked the question on the CDC blog, "Where do zombies come from, and why do they love eating brains so much?" The article went on to imagine, "Zombies would take over entire countries, roaming city streets eating anything living that got in their way." The proliferation of this idea has led many people to wonder: How do I prepare for a zombie apocalypse?

That's where the CDC got to drive home the message about stockpiling adequate food and water, determining a meeting site for family members, having important papers and documents collected and ready to go, and so on. It's a punch list of items that apply as much to a zombie apocalypse as, say, a pandemic (see Figure 13.9). Or a flood or earthquake. In fact, the CDC timed the post to coincide with the beginning of the hurricane season.

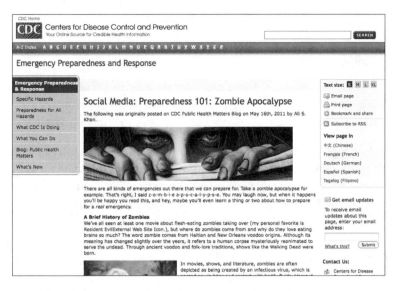

Figure 13.9   *Are you prepared for when zombies take over?*

Did it work? A CDC spokesperson said the organization gets an average of 1,000 to 3,000 visits to a web post. Prior to the zombie post, its most successful blog post saw about 10,000 visits. When the zombie apocalypse post went up, 60,000 visits brought down the organization's servers, and the campaign was a trending topic on Twitter that appeared on major blogs and in nationally syndicated news stories.

According to the CDC, the campaign was designed to reach a young, media-savvy demographic that the agency had not been able to capture previously. And it did. Someone at the CDC obviously has (ahem) brains.

If there's a lesson to be learned from where advertising leaves off and content marketing begins, it's that the content dimension goes deeper. It tells stories. It offers more information, entertainment, education. Rather than be limiting to a square, or a rectangle, or a mere 30 or 60 seconds, the content component to an advertising campaign offers an audience the opportunity to *voluntarily do more.*

That's an opportunity for advertisers that's too valuable to ignore when creating advertising campaigns. Some tactics they might consider to help readers, listeners, or viewers go deeper into their campaigns include these:

> "If there's a lesson to be learned from where advertising leaves off and content marketing begins, it's that the content dimension goes deeper."

- Provide a link to a relevant website in the ad.

- Include social media links and calls-to-action in the ad (follow us on Twitter, Facebook, and so on).

- Include QR codes for mobile users that provide deeper information (operating hours, for example) or special offers. (A QR, or "quick response" code, is a type of bar code scannable by a mobile device.)

If an ad captures attention, it's an opportunity for more content than an ad can possibly provide: Watch the video, download the whitepaper, subscribe for more information and updates. Content marketing will never replace good old-fashioned advertising, but it can certainly richly embellish it.

14

Content Marketing for Live Events

"Content marketers who are looking for new sources of content can generate a veritable geyser of invaluable content."

Content begets content, which is why content marketing and live events, online or offline, go hand-in-hand. Content marketing is an excellent way to market events, which, after all, are about providing content. Content marketers who are looking for new sources of content can generate a veritable geyser of invaluable content. This is true of any event—conferences, seminars, webinars, or trade shows— that can be leveraged in real time and can be parceled out in different formats and in varying channels over time.

I have broken down potential activities into three phases: before, during, and after the event in question. In other words:

- Content to encourage interest and attendance
- Content that publicizes the goings-on at the event itself
- Content generated by the event that can be spun off into other channels.

Before: Building Buzz and Interest

Ten or fifteen years ago, email was the de facto way to market an event. Although email still plays a critical role (particularly if you have a strong and responsive list), the plethora of content channels available to marketers at little to no cost create new ways to market content with content. These channels allow you to build buzz in advance of an event, to harness engagement before opening day, and to provide tantalizing previews of the coming attractions, from events on the main stage to highlights of a convention's trade show floor.

Hashtags—A Critical Underpinning

A foundational part of content event marketing is creating a unique hashtag and publicizing it from the get-go in all event materials. Hypothetically, this year's New York Auto Show hashtag could be, for example, NYAS12.

You want the hashtag to be short and unique, and you want it to be on all digital content associated with the event. For example:

- As a tag on blog entries.

- As a hashtag on Twitter (with the # sign, of course, so it would be rendered #NYAS12). See Figure 14.1.

- As part of the title or description of all multimedia materials, from photos to videos to podcasts.

Figure 14.1   *Your event hashtag also should be used as a Twitter hashtag.*

The purpose of a hashtag is to make any content related to an event (whether you created it) available and accessible to all comers—and searchers. Event hashtags (of course, hashtags have many other uses beyond events) organize and aggregate disparate material that's related to the same thing, such as the New York Auto Show.

The hashtag provides a window onto all the content and media that's created, discussed, passed along, and uploaded around the event in question. Hashtags make content organized and accessible, whether pre- or post event.

Social Media Channels

The advantages of having a Facebook event page are numerous. Facebook event pages provide a way to connect to prospective attendees and to announce updates to programs and schedules, as well as parties and special events. Facebook's functionality includes the ability to send public or private invitations to the main event or to smaller gatherings within the context of a larger conference. When people respond, invitations that are public are displayed on their own Facebook page, which in turn helps spread the word among their individual network of contacts.

Besides allowing posting of photos and videos about the event or its speakers or program updates, Facebook can be used for engagement.

ad:tech, a major conference for digital advertisers, asks questions of its users on Facebook and polls its audience about whether new conference elements should be continued (see Figure 14.2).

Figure 14.2   *ad:tech uses its Facebook community to help shape its conferences.*

It goes without saying that a Twitter account created specifically for your event serves many of these same purposes, as can a blog. An event YouTube channel is also very common these days. As shown in Figure 14.3, these can go quite deep, featuring photos, pre-interviews with speakers (audio, video, or plain old text), and offers for discount admission, and even attendee testimonials can be leveraged by all these platforms.

Figure 14.3   *A YouTube event channel.*

During: Building Engagement

Content marketing by no means stops when an event begins. Content can be collected and harnessed to build audience and attendee engagement during an event, as well as warehoused to roll out post event, to contribute to ongoing content marketing initiatives.

While your event is taking place, you should continue using the same social media channels that you used to publicize and build buzz for the event. In the tech sector, it's common (if not *de rigeur*) to liveblog sessions. What are the speakers saying about burning industry issues? Push out videos and photos. Snag people in the speaker room or in the hallway to capture video interviews that can be published in near-real time. Collect testimonials from attendees. Blogs can cover nearly every aspect of a trade show; some bloggers even keep their audience up to date on the swag and premiums handed out at tradeshow booths. Publish photos of people schmoozing at parties. (Nothing gets people's attention more than a photo of them pushed live to the Web.)

All legitimate forms of content should, of course, be labeled with the event hashtag. Don't forget to search for content published under that hashtag. Odds are the audience will be blogging and tweeting the proceedings as well.

Consider building a mobile app that helps attendees navigate the event. An exemplary example is SXSW GO, an app that helps thousands of visitors to Austin, Texas, get the most out of the massive South By Southwest festival every year (see

Figure 14.4). Some of the app's features include the ability to build a personal schedule for the event. Users can search or browse the entire event list or create and save filters based on category, subcategory, track, and venue.

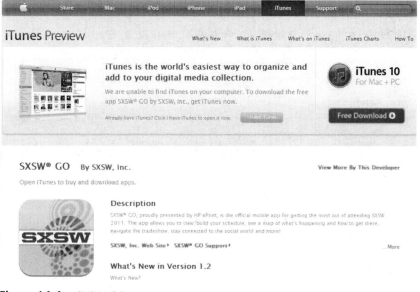

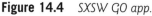

Figure 14.4   *SXSW GO app.*

The app also includes a map that displays what's going on and how to get there. The tradeshow can be searched or browsed for exhibitors, and there's a built-in link to major social media sites such as Facebook, Gowalla, and Twitter, so users can track all the content being created around the festival by other attendees.

Keeping people in touch with an event as it happens—even people who are unable to attend—provides a great window on your business's concerns, style, and personality. This can pay dividends into the future.

After: You've Got Content!

Hosting or even attending a professional event can have lots of purposes: marketing a business, nurturing leads, connecting with clients, and making new connections. For content marketers, an event is also a rich opportunity to harvest content that can be pushed out through a variety of channels and presented in a multitude of ways.

Those who are constantly on the hunt for new ideas for content can find goldmines at events, conferences, and tradeshows.

Bearing in mind the cardinal rule to always, always use hashtags, an obvious way to feature event content is to make presentations publicly accessible on Slideshare (see Figure 14.5). This free site hosts PowerPoint and other presentations online or via download. Obviously, aside from announcing that presentations will be available on Slideshare after an event, blogs and other social media links discussing presentation content can link to the original presentation.

Figure 14.5 *Make your presentations publicly available on Slideshare.*

Post-event is also the time to assess content that was created, generated, and harvested at the event. It's also the time to develop an editorial calendar to roll it out in different channels and in different formats over time. Do you have a video interview with an industry luminary? By all means, post it on YouTube, and link to the video from a blog or Facebook page. Also consider transcribing the spoken word, which creates extra SEO value; search engines can only "read" text, not video. Then use that written-word format for a blog entry, an eBook chapter, or a newsletter article.

Although some content generated by a live event will be hot-off-the-presses newsworthy, other elements will range from topical to evergreen. Parcel it out accordingly. Events are a rich source of content that in the future will be graded on success metrics. Those metrics will take into account leads generated or deals closed, as well as the quality and quantity of content generated for ongoing marketing initiatives.

"Those who are constantly on the hunt for new ideas for content can find goldmines at events, conferences, and tradeshows."

15

Content and Customer Service

"All content marketing is customer service."

In a very real sense, all content marketing is customer service. The very basis of any content plan is to serve the needs of varying customer constituencies: to educate and inform them, to answer their questions throughout the buying cycle, and to help them better understand and use the products and services you're offering.

So how can digital content best address customer service issues? The most strategic approach is three-pronged:

- *Anticipate and address needs in advance.*

- *Create feedback mechanisms so new issues can be folded into the support process.*

- *Develop a one-to-one response process to respond to individual queries.*

Not surprisingly, each of these approaches comes complete with its own set of challenges and layers of complexity.

Anticipating and Addressing Need

Anticipating and addressing customer needs is something that electronics manufacturers strive to address. That's understandable for products that are inherently complex, but other businesses can learn lessons from the varying levels of support that companies such as Sony provide on their website. Better yet, that support is surrounded by content (see Figure 15.1).

Figure 15.1   *Sony's support site is rich in content options to help customers solve their problems without having to contact customer service reps.*

For each product Sony sells, there are 10 different paths customers can take on the Sony website to address their support needs:

- Download drivers.

- Download software.

- Get answers to FAQs (frequently asked questions).

- Read news and alerts.

- Watch automated tutorials.

- Get information about how to obtain a repair.

- Use a contact link for reaching support personnel.

- Register a product.

- Shop in the Sony store.

- Visit the user forum.

Navigate over to Dell's customer support, and you're immediately channeled onto an appropriate page for your particular needs, whether you're an individual user, a small business, or a large enterprise (see Figure 15.2).

Figure 15.2 *Dell segments its support by customer type to help users find the content they need faster and more easily.*

Sony and Dell have done an excellent job of anticipating customer needs and creating content to address the needs of multiple customer segments. Not only is the support based on user type (are you an individual or a huge corporation?), but the navigation and information architecture also enable users to self-serve and zero in on the type of content they prefer. You may want to read a manual. You might plan to download a PDF, while I prefer to absorb that knowledge by watching a video. Sony knows this and offers various content alternatives.

What's the value in creating deep, rich customer support content in multiple media formats? Plenty. In addition to addressing customer needs with the service they expect and demand, creating easily navigable and accessible support content reduces customer support calls and emails. This is particularly true if you want repeat business, which we all know is much more valuable than one-time buyers. All of this translates directly into content ROI.

Create Feedback Mechanisms

Occasionally, there's a company that actually encourages customers to contact them. Zappos has built a successful business on exactly this high-touch model. If you mouse over Help in the Zappos navigation bar, the call-to-action is a highly unusual Talk to Us pop-up (see Figure 15.3). This pop-up encourages customer calls, emails, and live chats. However, even the Talk to Us pop-up links to a fairly extensive FAQ page that contains plenty of text content addressing the questions that Zappos phone reps are used to answering (see Figure 15.4).

Figure 15.3   *Believe it or not, Zappos actually wants to talk to its customers.*

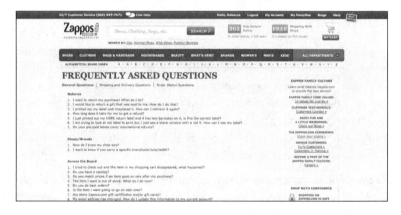

Figure 15.4   *Zappos still provides online FAQs for those who want them.*

Creating and publishing content around the calls and emails coming into a support center is only one aspect of creating feedback mechanisms that continually inform and lead to the creation of new customer support content going forward. Monitoring customer support forums for issues and problems that crop up with new and old products is another way of learning what types of content should be added to FAQs, manuals, videos, and other support channels.

External listening is critical, too. Although customers will often raise issues with a company directly, they'll also air problems, fixes, and issues in general elsewhere on the Web: on Facebook, via Twitter, in user groups, and on discussion boards. It's likely that customers (and prospects) are catching wind of customer service issues "in the wild," rather than in relatively safer confines of your own website. In fact, while writing this chapter, I was also troubleshooting an issue with my Kindle. I found quite a lively discussion from other users having the same problem on www.kindleboards.com, along with shared information on how customers were resolving the issue with Amazon. Amazon is obviously paying attention. The moment I contacted Amazon about the issue, it said it was aware of it and unhesitatingly sent a replacement unit.

That goes beyond great customer service. It's customer service that positively resonates in user-generated content across the Web, not just in the company's own customer service content. By monitoring those external posts and conversations, a company can sense an impending problem or even a crisis. Better yet, a company can then take steps to address and combat the problem with content—and eventually, even with better products. Of course, this will only happen if the feedback loop extends back far enough into the organization, as it should.

Creating One-on-One Communication

The final step in addressing customer service–oriented content is one-on-one communication. No matter how good, how thorough, how many channels, and how multimedia-driven your customer service content is, your organization is going to have to talk to, email, tweet, or otherwise address service concerns individually. It's private communication, but these days even private communication between companies and customers frequently comes into the spotlight. Customers have become as eager to "review" customer service in public forums as they are accustomed to reviewing their latest purchase on Amazon. Customers are also eager to vent customer service complaints in public forums such as Facebook and Twitter.

An important first step in customer service is an email auto-response message to customer inquiries and complaints that is sent to a customer as soon as customer service is contacted. This message should, of course, be composed in the voice of the organization and clearly outline how and when the customer can expect a personal response to his or her issue. It may, for example, promise a response within 12 hours, or within one business day—a reasonable timeframe that won't leave the customer hanging or wondering if they've sent an email inquiry into the void. Naturally, it's incumbent on the company to actually deliver on that promise of help within the promised timeframe.

> "Customers are also eager to vent customer service complaints in public forums such as Facebook and Twitter."

Of course, customer service has bled into broader channels than email. Twitter has become an important customer service channel, and many companies now have dedicated teams in place who spend their time addressing customer service issues in the channel.

One early Twitter customer service success story is Comcast. The company's reputation in customer service was abysmal; no-show repairmen, unresolved service outages, and billing complaints created a firestorm of negative verging on vitriolic complaints on Twitter and in other social media channels. Frank Eliason, a Comcast employee, put together a team that started addressing customer complaints on Twitter (see Figure 15.5). "How can I help?" was an oft-tweeted response to complaints about service. The teams also supplied phone numbers, email addresses, and escalated and routed issues to the proper departments in the company.

Figure 15.5   *ComcastCares started as a grassroots effort by one small group of Comcast employees.*

The now-often imitated initiative was, and remains, a runaway success. Twitter customer service is clearly not a solution that scales well, but although Comcast is a nationwide company with hundreds of thousands of subscribers, it did solve numerous customer services issues nationally and created enormous goodwill in the process. It's a public relations coup: customers began to believe a monolithic conglomerate actually *does* care.

Eliason has since left the company, but @ComcastCares boasts more than 52,000 Twitter followers and counting. And the model has been imitated (see Figure 15.6) by companies large and small, in industries ranging from automotive (Ford) to financial services (American Express).

Figure 15.6 *Many companies, including Ford, have imitated the ComcastCares initiative.*

16

Content and Reputation Management

"The practice of online reputation management is based overwhelmingly on one practice: content marketing."

What is online reputation management? The answer is twofold:

- *It's the practice of monitoring the online reputation of a person, brand, product, or business.*

- *It's the practice of addressing negative mentions, either by eliminating or suppressing them or by decreasing their visibility on search engine results pages by pushing them lower; for example, it might involve making the negative content appear on page 15 of a Google results page rather than on page 1 or 2.*

Online reputation has become a thriving business. Many companies and products offer services to manage online reputations. Although reputation management sometimes involves requests or demands that negative content be removed from the Web, doing so is neither a reliable nor an effective strategy. The practice of online reputation management is based overwhelmingly on one practice: content marketing.

At the most fundamental level, search engines are designed to do one thing: find and prioritize online content based on the words or phrases used in search queries. Long before the term "online reputation management" was coined, marketers were advised to Google the names associated with their companies, brands, products, and executives, plus the qualifier "sucks," to learn if they were being dissed online and why.

An example is the infamous "miserable failure" Googlebombing case study. In 2003, back in the George W. Bush administration, a loose, but large, fraternity of websites linked the term "miserable failure" to point to the then-president's official White House biography web page. It stayed that way for four years, until Google retooled its search algorithm to counteract the practice. But, as illustrated in Figure 16.1, the meme lives on.

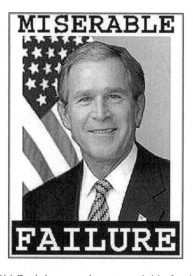

Figure 16.1   *George W. Bush became the poster child of online reputation problems when he became forever linked with the phrase "miserable failure" in search results.*

That was back in the days before social media. In 2003, it still was relatively difficult to build a web page or site to air complaints and share them with friends, members of your business network, or the entire universe of Internet users.

No longer. Consumers complain across the social web sphere: on blogs, forums, social networking sites such as Facebook and LinkedIn, Twitter, and YouTube videos, to name only a few of the channels readily available to anyone with an Internet connection. Own a local business? Consumers are reviewing you on Citysearch, Yelp, Zagat.com, and the local business listings at Google, Bing, and Yahoo. Selling products? Consumers can easily review your wares on Amazon or virtually any other major ecommerce site. In fact, many of these sites have social media links that let consumers push their opinions from a product page straight to Facebook or Twitter.

Monitoring—and addressing—online reputation issues boils down to search engine optimization (SEO). Creating, disseminating, and promoting strong, credible, positive content is pretty much the only weapon at a marketer's disposal.

Online reputation management starts with having a content strategy and content marketing already in place. You don't want to wait until there's a fire blazing to assemble the tools you need to douse the blaze. Rather, not only do you want those tools in place, you also want to have already constructed fortifications in the form of plenty of optimized content on the Web in general, as well as on blogs, social media, and social networking sites.

> "Creating, disseminating, and promoting strong, credible, positive content is pretty much the only weapon at a marketer's disposal."

It's also critically important that all online content and digital communications are optimized for search. This includes public relations (PR), marketing, and investor relations, as well as any other digital content available on the Web, anywhere. Optimized text, images, audio, and video results in more content showing up in search engine results pages.

Don't be fooled that after your content elements are in place, you can forget about them. Content marketing, like SEO, is an ongoing process. You'll always have to continue what journalists have long called "feeding the beast."

Reviews won't always be positive, and 100% of customers will never be happy 100% of the time. Online reputation management isn't about obliterating any negative mention or association made with your organization, but about mitigating those negative results with strong, positive, visible, and consistent content.

Crisis Management

As any politician caught with his pants down (literally) can attest, reputation issues can strike suddenly and without warning. Online, such attacks can be vicious and literally take down careers and businesses in a manner of days or weeks, often in a highly visible way.

Some online crises are just destined to end badly. It's nearly impossible to conceive of a strategy that would retroactively restore the reputation of a married member of congress who was discovered to be sending inappropriate photos of himself to young women on Twitter, for example.

Dell learned this the hard way in 2005 when A-list blogger Jeff Jarvis, frustrated with the company's refusal to repair or replace his defective computer, published an open letter to CEO Michael Dell on his blog, BuzzMachine. Immediately, it became one of the most widely read, discussed, linked-to, and viral articles on the Web— ever. Every major newspaper and magazine in the country ran the story of what came to be dubbed "Dell Hell." That's when Dell (the company *and* the CEO) sat up and took notice (see Figure 16.2).

Figure 16.2 *You can believe that Dell went through a very time and money- consuming type of hell trying to undo the "Dell Hell" meme.*

It was a slow and painful evolution, but Dell revamped its customer service and began both blogging and reaching out to bloggers. When Twitter was released, Dell was one of the first companies with a presence on the platform. Now, the company has at least nine different Facebook pages and an equal number of blogs. It also runs various community sites for customers.

It took a full-blown crisis to get Dell to respond. After it did, however, it quickly realized the value of entering into a dialogue with its customers, and not just the ones of Jeff Jarvis's stature. Does Dell still have customer service issues? Certainly. But the fact that the company is committed to continually publishing content that discusses its concerns, challenges, innovations, and efforts both in business and in the communities it serves goes far to mitigate customer dissatisfaction.

It's not all about pushing bad search results into the background. A strong content marketing plan can all but ensure that the next time there's a problem, it won't erupt into a firestorm.

All this didn't happen at Dell overnight. For several years now, the company has been making new hires and training existing employees in social media and cus- tomer conversations. Companies that haven't already taken these measures are beginning to wish that they had, particularly when they confront a crisis precipi- tated by a highly digitally sophisticated opponent.

Case in point: Greenpeace vs. Nestlé. In 2010, Greenpeace launched a campaign consisting of a website and a Facebook page protesting Nestlé's sourcing of the palm oil used in Kit-Kat candy bars. The oil was being harvested from—and destroying— Indonesian rainforests, pushing orangutans further toward the brink of extinction and threatening the livelihoods of local residents.

Destroying rainforests and driving species into extinction is no one's idea of corporate responsibility, but Nestlé was ill-prepared for the angry onslaught of Facebook protesters, particularly when people started to replace their profile pictures with a Kit-Kat logo (see Figure 16.3) modified to read "Killer."

Figure 16.3 *When you think candy bar, its manufacturer doesn't want you to associate the product with the eradication of endangered rainforests and orangutans.*

That's when things started to really fall apart. Nestlé's social media "voices," most likely outside PR people or untrained interns, got a note from legal and started, amid a substantive discussion about sustainability, to hand out take-down notices.

An excerpt from one ill-advised interaction is show here.

> **Nestle** *To repeat: we welcome your comments, but please don't post using an altered version of any of our logos as your profile pic—they will be deleted.*
>
> **Paul Griffin** *Hmm, this comment is a bit "Big Brotherish" isn't it? I'll have whatever I like as my logo pic thanks! And if it's altered, it's no longer your logo is it!*
>
> **Nestle @Paul Griffin** *That's a new understanding of intellectual property rights. We'll muse on that. You can have what you like as your profile picture. But if it's an altered version of any of our logos, we'll remove it from this page.*
>
> **Paul Griffin** *Not sure you're going to win friends in the social media space with this sort of dogmatic approach. I understand that you're on your back-foot due to various issues not excluding Palm Oil but Social Media is about embracing your market, engaging and having a conversation rather than preaching! Read www.cluetrain.com and rethink!*

Nestlé stock began to plummet, and the story (predictably) hit the mainstream media. A few days into the debacle, Nestlé changed the corporate statement on its Facebook page to read: "Social media: as you can see we're learning as we go. Thanks for the comments."

Lessons learned? Opponents such as Greenpeace are incredibly well organized. They're Web-, media-, and PR-savvy—as are many individual web users out there. Companies must be well prepared with content, PR-savvy, and the ability to create the right kind of content and deliver it in the appropriate voice. Threatening to sue your customers is never a good strategy (just ask the RIAA). Nor is nitpicking over a logo or copyright issues when lives are—literally—at stake.

Nestlé could certainly have anticipated this campaign. Unilever and Kraft had already stopped their dealings with the Indonesian supplier, at Greenpeace's behest. So in addition to not leaving their social media communications and content to unseasoned and junior staff, Nestlé could have rehearsed scenarios it must have known were coming, even if it didn't exactly know the form they would take.

> "Sometimes, reputation management is as simple a matter as turning lemons into lemonade."

It would also have helped Nestlé to have developed, in advance, relationships that could have strengthened its position. Nestlé eventually did capitulate on its palm oil sourcing. Reportedly, the company had been investigating new sources all along and planned to stop buying from the Indonesian supplier. Nestlé could have backed this up with content, such as this:

- Blog entries from company executives with documentation of the research it was conducting

- Interviews with experts on sustainability

- Interviews with supply chain management experts

- Interviews with product sourcers

All this would have provided a wellspring of *substantive* content Nestlé could have used in its public discussions with protesters. Instead, the (presumed) memo from legal took precedence, with unnecessarily disastrous results.

In closing this chapter, let's look at a final and rather unorthodox case study. This one hails from Austin, Texas, home of the Alamo Drafthouse Cinema, one of the most respected arthouse chains in the country.

The Alamo Drafthouse ejected—without a refund—a customer who, despite a posted rule, was texting on her cell phone during a film. Incensed, the customer left a long, vitriolic, and obscenity-laden message on the theatre's voicemail. The Alamo converted the message into a YouTube video. In three days, the video went mega-viral with more than three million views and a tidal wave of positive responses from cinema-goers everywhere. The story made CNN and other major media outlets.

This customer's attempt to censure the Alamo for enforcing its policy instead turned the cinema into a hero. The Alamo recognized the opportunity to turn a complaint into content that spoke to the frustrations of filmgoers everywhere who are faced with rude behavior.

Sometimes, reputation management is as simple a matter as turning lemons into lemonade (see Figure 16.4).

Figure 16.4   *Remember the Alamo! The theatre chain made news and earned accolades by turning a customer complaint into a testimonial to its integrity.*

17

User-Generated Content

"It's no wonder that content creators feel they could use some help—and they have it, in the form of users."

Content can be a wildly effective marketing tool, but content doesn't create itself. Stories, videos, blog posts, Twitter tweets, photos, surveys, whitepapers, and eBooks are just the tip of the iceberg. No sooner have you created new content then it's time to go back to the drawing board and create, create again. Content is work-intensive and time-consuming, not to mention expensive.

It's no wonder that content creators feel they could use some help—and they have it, in the form of users.

They don't call it user-generated content for nothing. More than 82 million people in the United States created online content back in 2008. That number is expected to swell to nearly 115 million by 2013, according to research firm eMarketer.

Most content creators are on social networks such as Facebook posting photos or links. Many users review products and services on retail sites, such as Amazon or Netflix, or on "places" sites such as Yelp, Zagat.com, and a host of others. There's also a rapidly growing population participating in much deeper activities such as blogging, curating, and organizing content on sites such as Digg, StumbleUpon and Delicious, or uploading their own videos (see Figure 17.1).

US User-Generated Content Creators, by Content Type, 2008-2013 (millions)

	2008	2009	2010	2011	2012	2013
User-generated video	15.4	18.1	20.6	22.7	24.9	27.2
Social networking	71.3	79.7	87.7	94.7	100.1	105.3
Blogs	21.2	23.9	26.7	28.5	30.2	32.1
Virtual worlds	11.6	13.9	15.4	16.9	18.4	19.9
User-generated content creators	**82.5**	**88.8**	**95.3**	**101.7**	**108.0**	**114.5**

Source: eMarketer, January 2009

100883   www.e**Marketer**.com

Figure 17.1   *Tools are cheap and getting cheaper, so is the level of skill required to create digital content in every channel.*

Some 71 million people created content on social networks in 2008, back when they were relatively new. At the same time, 21 million blogged, and 15 million uploaded videos (see Figure 17.2).

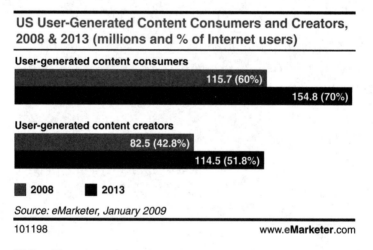

Figure 17.2   *The easier it becomes to create content, the more consumers will create it—particularly as another generation of "digital natives" grows up.*

It's getting ever easier for consumers (and business professional, too, of course) to create and publish content—just as it is for businesses. And frequently, the content they produce is about businesses. The products they buy and use, the food they eat, the service providers they research, their vacation activities, and the books, movies, and DVDs they consume are just the tip of the iceberg.

Although opening up content marketing to consumer-generated content necessitates relinquishing (or at least sharing) control over messaging, there are strong and compelling reasons to do so. Worldwide, web users showed close to a 50% increase in their trust of social network contacts giving product recommendations, and a 21% increase for microblog contacts (see Figure 17.3). Meanwhile, "professional" sources of information such as newspapers and TV (and presumably, the advertising they carry) barely gained any trust over the same period (see Figure 17.4).

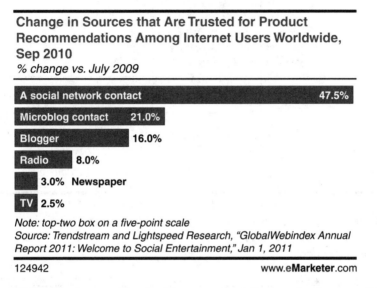

Change in Sources that Are Trusted for Product Recommendations Among Internet Users Worldwide, Sep 2010
% change vs. July 2009

A social network contact	47.5%
Microblog contact	21.0%
Blogger	16.0%
Radio	8.0%
3.0% Newspaper	
TV 2.5%	

Note: top-two box on a five-point scale
Source: Trendstream and Lightspeed Research, "GlobalWebindex Annual Report 2011: Welcome to Social Entertainment," Jan 1, 2011

124942   www.e**Marketer**.com

Figure 17.3   *People are gaining trust for recommendations coming from people in their social networks. Data courtesy of eMarketer.*

Trust is critical, which is why marketers must learn to invest trust in those who create content around their products and services. A survey of top marketing executives conducted in 2011 by Bazaarvoice/The CMO Club found that 93% of chief marketing officers (CMOs) plan on using some form of user-generated content to inform product and service decisions. As you can see in Figure 17.5, the top forms of user-generated content that marketers used in 2010 include customer stories (59%), product suggestions or ideas (54%), polling (49%), and customer reviews (47%).

"Trust is critical, which is why marketers must learn to invest trust in those who create content around their products and services."

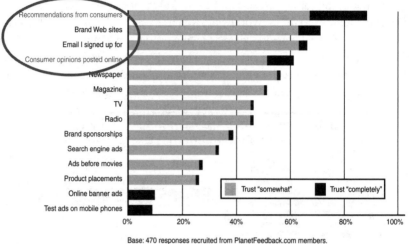

"Indicate your overall level of trust in the following forms of advertising."

Base: 470 responses recruited from PlanetFeedback.com members.
Source: Forrester Research, Inc. and Intelliseek.

Figure 17.4   *Conversely, newspaper and TV have barely gained any trust.*

User-Generated Content Used by CMOs Worldwide to Shape Decisions About Their Company's Products or Services, 2010 & 2011
% of respondents

	2010	2011
Customer stories about product/service	59.4%	77.7%
Product suggestions/ideas	53.7%	70.9%
Polling	48.6%	77.1%
Ratings and reviews	46.9%	70.3%
Forums	42.9%	74.3%
Presales Q&A	29.7%	32.0%
Twitter comments	22.9%	53.7%
Other	2.9%	4.6%
Don't know	2.3%	3.4%
None of the above	10.9%	7.4%

Note: n=175
Source: Bazaarvoice and The CMO Club, "CMOs on Social Marketing Plans for 2011," provided to eMarketer; eMarketer calculations, Jan 27, 2011

124604   www.**eMarketer**.com

Figure 17.5   *Customer stories were the main form of user-generated content used by marketers in 2010, with production suggestions/ideas, polling, and customer reviews following right behind. Data source: eMarketer.*

Soliciting Ideas

Some companies have launched entire websites to encourage customer ideas and participation. MyStarbucksIdea is an early example of a digital suggestion box on steroids. Starbucks customers can go to the site to submit ideas around products, store decor, new uses for the Starbucks loyalty card...anything Starbucks related (see Figure 17.6). Site users can comment on and vote for their favorite ideas.

Figure 17.6   *Have an idea you want to share with Starbucks? Visit MyStarbucksIdea.*

Dell Computer applies that same notion to its business with IdeaStorm, a forum for customer suggestions around its technology products and the ways Dell services and markets its offerings (see Figure 17.7).

Figure 17.7   *Dells' IdeaStrom is a forum for customer suggestions regarding its technologies and products.*

Even Kotex launched a website, UByKotex.com, asking customers to "Ban the Bland," or put an end to plain white sanitary napkins (see Figure 17.8). It's a suggestion site, but it's also a design competition in which the winners get a chance to share their designs and work alongside designer Patricia Field. According to the company's agency, Organic, the initiative resulted in a 10% jump in Kotex sales.

Figure 17.8   *Kotex offered visitors a chance to do away with plain, white sanitary napkins.*

Customer stories also add authenticity to brand messages. Many leading hotel chains now solicit customer photos and travel recommendations for local destinations. Amazon invites users to submit their own product photos to expand on the manufacturer-supplied product shots standard on ecommerce sites.

One particularly brave invitation to customers to tell their stories came from Miracle Whip, the ersatz mayonnaise. Recognizing that consumers either love the stuff or hate it, it invited users to submit videos to a YouTube channel explaining, in their own, unscripted words, why they're lovers or haters of the condiment. Comments range from, "My grandma makes the best potato salad with Miracle Whip!" to "I'd rather die than eat it!" Users are also invited to love or hate the product on Facebook.

Miracle Whip understands that everybody isn't going to love everything all the time, and nothing siphons authenticity out of a message faster than portraying things in too rosy a light.

Just five or so years ago, sites resisted adding user reviews of products and services. Fear of negative feedback is understandable, but that fear must be overcome. Negative reviews (like positive ones) help in buying decisions and create trust. User-generated content is, after all, about real people, not marketing-speak.

Moreover, Yelp has found that 85% of its reviews are positive, and Bazaarvoice says 80% of its user ratings are four or five stars. Any ecommerce merchant who runs reviews on its site will tell you it increases sales—as well as search engine optimization (SEO). Users often use the same language to discuss products that searchers use when seeking those same products.

In fact, the online retail clients of consumer-review provider, Bazaarvoice, never found more than a 3% overlap between the search terms in its review content and the terms it actually uses in its own product content.

In addition to sharing stories, polling, surveys, ratings, reviews, and product suggestions, companies can engage directly with customers through user-generated content. By responding to their comments on Twitter and on blog posts, or in communities and social networks, organizations can demonstrate that they care, are listening, and are interested in the conversations customers are having about and around them.

18

Content Distribution and Dissemination

"If consumers don't see/hear/watch/listen to it, it won't make a sound."

Creating great, persuasive, educational, entertaining, informative, and compelling content is important, but it isn't enough. It is critically important to get content "out there," to online and other digital channels. You must develop strategies for content distribution and dissemination that will get your content in front of its target audience as effectively and with as much visibility as possible.

Publishing content on a website, on a blog, or on a social network can indeed be effective, but it shouldn't stop there. A strong distribution/dissemination strategy creates opportunities to greatly amplify the impact and the reach of the content. It's the tree falling in the woods theory, as applied to content marketing. If consumers don't see/hear/watch/listen to it, it won't make a sound.

Additionally, publishing, and publicizing content on additional platforms, such as social networks, websites, and other digital media channels, regardless of what they are, automatically conveys search engine optimization (SEO) benefits. Not only will content be more findable to its intended audience when it appears on more platforms, it will be more findable by search engines. Links will be created to and from your website or relevant web presence that can help boost visibility for the piece of content in question and possibly for a site or blog in general.

Finally, maximizing the channels where content appears increases its chances for viral pass-alongs. But it also increases the chances that members of a social or business network, an email list, or subscribers to a newsletter or RSS feed are exposed to the content. Better yet, making content available to multiple channels increases the chances that people seeing the content will virally distribute it to their own lists of contacts, followers, or networks.

What follows are some best-practice strategies for getting content "out there."

Contribute

Certainly your own website, blog, Facebook page, and other content channels are taking up plenty of your time, as well they should. But that's no excuse for underestimating the value of contributing content to properties you don't own or control to increase visibility and gain new audiences you may not otherwise have attracted.

- **Publications**—A key component of contributed content is published bylined articles, editorials, or columns in relevant editorial publications (online or off). These can be industry, trade print or broadcast publications in your area of expertise. They also can be business journals, local news publications, or anything that's relevant to your business or goals. One of the strongest reasons to pursue this path is that editorial media outlets have editorial controls. The information they publish automatically conveys a higher level of authority and quality given there are hurdles to overcome in the editorial process.

- **Blogs**—The same path can be taken with relevant blogs (many of which have higher levels of readership than more "traditional" publications). Again, guest blogging on relevant sites creates more awareness and can build new audience segments. Guest blogging also creates valuable links back to your own site or content. Don't forget to reciprocate by inviting guest bloggers to contribute to your own blog, as well.

Finally, keep track of content you publish on external sites. Blogs and online newspapers and magazines almost always have comment sections. As an author, you have a responsibility to monitor the discussions around your contribution and to contribute to the discussion around the issues you raised.

Promote

Go social when contributed content is published, whether on a blog or in a more traditional news outlet. There's absolutely no excuse not to promote your content. For instance, tweet a teasing heading and a link, or add summaries and links to social networking sites and to news aggregation and social bookmarking sites such as Digg, Delicious, and StumbleUpon. In addition to creating and amplifying awareness for your own content, you're helping to drive traffic to the source that published your content contribution. They'll appreciate it.

As discussed in Chapter 11, "Content and SEO," the value of an online press release has increased exponentially online. Press release that go out over wire services create additional links, boost SEO, and are often picked up automatically by portal news sites (not just editorial sites and blogs). Disseminating content online, therefore, involves rethinking what's newsworthy in terms of making a formal press announcement. Moreover, archiving news releases on a website or on a digital media center creates internal links that boost content visibility. So when you've created and published content on a third-party site, be proud of it—support it with a press release! Of course, there's always the chance the press release will serve its more traditional purpose: getting that content noticed, picked up, and linked to by yet another news source.

Syndicate via RSS Feeds

It's likely that content is being published on a regular basis on several sections of your website or sites. Blogs, press releases, new product announcements, podcasts, and a YouTube channel are just a few examples of areas that are frequently or regularly updated. RSS (which stands for either rich site summary or really simple syndication—take your pick) allows newsreaders and aggregators to scrape headlines, summaries, and links off websites for syndication.

RSS has long been used to syndicate news content and financial information such as stock quotes. More recently, it's become standard operating procedure for blogs. Organizations are turning to RSS to issue events listings, project updates, and corporate announcements. There are RSS feeds that can track eBay listings, products on Amazon, packages sent via major courier services, project management activities, forum/listserve posts,

> "RSS is an invaluable tool for getting content out there, rather than simply building it and hoping they will come."

recently added downloads, search results, a book's revision history—you name it. If it's online, and particularly if it's frequently updated, it's almost certainly RSS-able. RSS is an invaluable tool for getting content out there, rather than simply building it and hoping they will come.

Make sure you push content, or links to content, out on social networks, forums and discussion sites. However, don't forget the old standards for content pushing, like good, old-fashioned email, which still works perfectly well both for announcements and newsletters with links back to online content.

There are also numerous ways to repurpose content from one channel into another. For example, a webinar can be recorded as a video and published on your own website or YouTube. Going further still, tools such as Tubemogul can push that same video to some 30 video sharing sites.

More ways to repurpose content are examined in Chapter 23, "Listening…and Responding."

19

Whose Job Is Content?

"You're at least as much a publisher as you are an advertiser."

Content marketing has been embraced by businesses large and small. They know there's far less of a need to buy media when they can create it themselves. They're aware that if you have a website, a blog, a YouTube channel, a Twitter presence, a Facebook page, or a host of other online offerings, you're at least as much a publisher as you are an advertiser.

But strategizing, creating, assessing, disseminating, evaluating, and monetizing content doesn't just happen by itself. Someone's got to actually do it.

How do organizations determine who that someone is? There are certainly plenty of roles and responsibilities that can oversee, or play a role in, content marketing. Here are just a few of the most obvious examples:

- Chief content officer/VP of content
- Chief marketing officer
- Everyone (or very nearly everyone)
- Content/editorial director
- Conversation/community director

- Blogger
- Social media guru
- Copywriter
- Copy editor
- Outside consultant(s)
- Public relations professional

Companies that really buy into content marketing are increasingly taking the "everyone" approach. At the very least, they're hiring a whole lot of people to be responsible for creating digital content because its worth has been solidly demonstrated.

Zappos is one such organization. It started testing video product demonstrations in late 2008. A year later, it was producing 60–100 videos per day, with a goal of 50,000 by the end of this year. To that end, the company is upping its full-time video production staff of 40, not to mention the scores of employees who appear in the majority of the demonstration spots.

The Zappos content team senior manager, Rico Nasol, has been quoted as saying the company sees conversion increase up to 30% on products that are accompanied by video.

Think this commitment to content is relevant only to business-to-consumer (B2C) companies? Think again. Rick Short heads marketing for Indium Corporation in northern New York State. As we learned in Chapter 1, "What's Content Marketing, Anyway?," his team publishes a staggering 73 blogs on the topic of soldering supplies. Each blog and blog entry is, in turn, translated into seven languages.

Seventy-three blogs on...*soldering supplies?*

"A lot of people have the same reaction you have," Rick will assure you. "They're surprised a topic like soldering would be worthy of this kind of social media attention. Bottom line is that's all I do. That's my job. This isn't arcane and weird. I'm surrounded by 600 colleagues who are really into it. We've dedicated our careers to it. These topics that we in our industry are consumed with are very rich, complex, and rewarding. The team is *bona fide*, qualified engineers. What a great marketing tool! Why would I hire anyone to rep me when the 'me' is better than anything out there?

"If I'd put someone between me and my readers, it would read like another press release. We went right to authentic and real. We've got to get rid of the Mad Men, take them out of the equation, and go to the market one engineer to another. These guys are smart. They're PhDs. We can't think we're impressing them in this old school, go-to-market style. I want you to be the one who speaks, who takes the picture, whose work is expressed in your own voice. They started seeing that I was sincere, and the customers sincerely appreciate it."

How did Short arrive at 73 blogs? That's the number of keywords he identified that the company's clients searched on when looking for Indium's products and services.

Clearly, when the job is creating lots of content, it helps to have lots of contributors. Yet putting someone at the helm of those initiatives is critical—as critical as putting an editor-in-chief in charge of everything published by a newspaper or magazine. Consistency, style, voice, adherence to mission, editorial judgment, and ethics are just a part of the role.

Joe Chernov is vice president of content marketing at Eloqua. He defines his own responsibilities thusly:

"My role is to identify content that will be valuable and share-worthy to the company's audience and to figure out how to procure that. Do you have resources in-house, the skill set, to collaborate with the demand team, then to distribute content through channels that make most sense?

"Clearly, when the job is creating lots of content, it helps to have lots of contributors."

"The aperture is set kind of wide regarding what content marketing is. In some ways, I wonder if companies that have a blog could check that 'content marketing blog' box and move on. They'll never do the real content marketing labor, which isn't just tweeting out headlines that are related to your industry, but instead creating substantive, share-worthy content that gets people to talk about you and spend time on their website and gets them to engage in the things you want them to engage in."

Okay, but Eloqua is a business-to-business (B2B) technology company, not an ecommerce player like Zappos. So how does Chernov measure the impact that the content he's creating and overseeing has on the bottom line? He admits it's not a clear equation but counters with a question: "How many shipwrecks did a lighthouse prevent?"

To assess the skill sets required in a chief content officer, Joe Pullizzi recently published a highly detailed job description template[1] (see the next section). It's so detailed, in fact, it's likely better used as a jumping-off point for modeling your own needs upon. It's a great point of departure for anyone working to design the skill sets they need for in-house content staff.

✉ *Note*

> See the following site, and adapt it to your organization's content marketing needs:
>
> http://blog.junta42.com/2011/05/chief-content-officer-job-description-sample-example-tempate/

---

1 Copyright Joe Pulizzi, The Content Marketing Institute; used with permission

Job Description: Chief Content Officer

Reports To

Chief executive officer/chief operating officer (smaller enterprise) or chief marketing officer/VP of marketing (larger enterprise)

Position Summary

The chief content officer (CCO) oversees all marketing content initiatives, both internal and external, across multiple platforms and formats to drive sales, engagement, retention, leads, and positive customer behavior.

This individual is an expert in all things related to content and channel optimization, brand consistency, segmentation and localization, analytics, and meaningful measurement.

The position collaborates with the departments of public relations, communications, marketing, customer service, IT, and human resources to help define both the brand story and the story as interpreted by the customer.

Responsibilities

Ultimately, the job of the CCO is to think like a publisher/journalist, leading the development of content initiatives in all forms to drive new and current business. This includes

- Ensuring all content is on-brand; consistent in terms of style, quality, and tone of voice; and optimized for search and user experience for all channels of content including online, social media, email, point of purchase, mobile, video, print, and in-person. This is to be done for each buyer persona within the enterprise.

- Mapping out a content strategy that supports and extends marketing initiatives, both short and long term, determining which methods work for the brand and why. Continuous evolvement of strategy is a must.

- Developing a functional content calendar throughout the enterprise verticals, and defining the owners in each vertical to particular persona groups.

- Supervising writers, editors, and content strategists; being an arbiter of best practices in grammar, messaging, writing, and style.

- Integrating content activities within traditional marketing campaigns.

- Conducting ongoing usability tests to gauge content effectiveness. Gathering data and handling analytics (or supervising those who do) and making recommendations based on those results. Working with owners of particular content to revise and measure particular content and marketing goals.

- Developing standards, systems, and best practices (both human and technological) for content creation, distribution, maintenance, content retrieval, and content repurposing, including the real-time implementation of content strategies.

- Leveraging market data to develop content themes/topics and execute a plan to develop the assets that support a point of view and educate customers that leads to critical behavioral metrics.

- Establishing work flow for requesting, creating, editing, publishing, and retiring content.

- Working with the technical team to implement an appropriate content management system (CMS).

- Conducting periodic competitive audits.

- Supervising the maintenance of content inventories and matrices.

- Ensuring a consistent global experience and implementing appropriate localization/translation strategies.

- Participating in the hiring and supervising of content/story leaders in all content verticals.

- Creating a strategy for developing SMS/MMS outreach and advertising apps and so on as needed.

- Working closely with company's chief design officer on all creative and branding initiatives to ensure a consistent message across channels.

Success Criteria

The CCO is measured on the continual improvement of customer nurturing and retention through storytelling, as well as the increase in new prospects into the enterprise through the consistent development and deployment of content to each persona group. Success criteria include

- Positive brand recognition and consistency across chosen published channels.

- An increase in defined customer engagement metrics (measured by users taking the desired action—that is, conversion, subscription, purchase, and so on).

- Website and social media traffic growth.

- Conversion metrics definition and growth.

- Social media positive sentiment metrics.

- Customer feedback and survey data.

- Increases in key search engine keyword rankings.

- A decrease in sales/buying cycles.

- Clearly defining content distribution during particular stages of the buying cycle (lead nurturing).

- Identifying up-sell and cross-sell opportunities through content analysis, and deploying content assets for higher conversion rates.

- Primary criteria for success are customer and employee affinity. Success is measured around lifetime customer value, customer satisfaction, and employee advocacy.

Experience and Education Required

- Bachelor's degree in English, journalism, public relations, or related communications field. MBA in marketing a plus.

- 10–15 years of experience as a respected leader in multichannel content creation (publishing, journalism, and so on).

- Experience with creating compelling messages for different target demographics. Crisis communications experience a plus.

- Expertise in all major business software applications (Adobe Creative Suite, Microsoft Office, and so on).

- HR-related experience, including hiring, managing, performance reviews, compensation packages, and so on required.

- Multilingual abilities (specifically Spanish and Chinese) a major plus.

- Audience development and subscription strategies experience a plus.

Skills Required

The CCO requires a combination marketing and publishing mindset, with the most important aspect being to think "customer first." In essence, the CCO is the corporate storyteller that must be empathetic toward the pain points of the customer. Specific skills required include

- Proven editorial skills. Outstanding command of the English (or primary customer) language.

- Training as a print or broadcast journalist with a "nose" for the story. Training in how to tell a story using words, images, or audio, and an understanding of how to create content that draws an audience. (It is critical that the CCO retain an "outsider's perspective" much like that of a journalist.)

- The ability to lead and inspire large teams of creative personnel and content creators to achieve company's stated goals.

- Skill at both long-form content creation and real-time (immediate) content creation and distribution strategies and tactics.

- The ability to think like an educator, intuitively understanding what the audience needs to know and how they want to consume it.

- A passion for new technology tools (aka, using the tools you preach about), and usage of those tools within your own blogs and social media outreach. Social DNA a plus!

- Clear articulation of the business goal behind the creation of a piece (or series) of content.

- Leadership skills required to define and manage a set of goals involving diverse contributors and content types.

- Project management skills to manage editorial schedules and deadlines within corporate and ongoing campaigns. Ability to work in a 24-hour project cycle utilizing teams or contractors in other countries.

- Familiarity with principles of marketing (and the ability to adapt or ignore them as dictated by data).

- Excellent negotiation and mediation skills.

- Incredible people skills.

- Basic technical understanding of HTML, XHTML, CSS, Java, web publishing, and Flash.

- Fluency in web analytics tools (Adobe Omniture, Google Analytics), social media marketing applications (HootSuite, Tweetdeck, and so on), and leading social media monitoring platforms (Radian6, and so on).

- A willingness to embrace change and to adapt strategies on the fly.

- Great powers of persuasion and presentation (Visio, PowerPoint).

- Experience creating a resource or library of content organized indicating SEO, translations, and version control.

- Continually learning the latest platforms, technology tools, and marketing solutions through partnerships.

- Able to screen out sales pitches and look for the relevant brand and customer story.

- Comfortable with acting as the company's spokesman and advocate via media appearances, interviews, sales calls, trade shows, and more.

20

How to Conduct a Content Audit

You can't know where you're going if you don't know where you are. You may think you know where you are, but without a thorough website content audit, it's likely you don't.

Why perform a content audit, which admittedly is a painstaking and exacting exercise? Lots of reasons.

- *It helps determine if digital content is relevant, both to customer needs and to the goals of the organization.*

- *It's a gauge for content accuracy and consistency.*

- *It points to the voice of the organization.*

- *It verifies your optimization for search.*

- *It determines whether technical frameworks, such as the content management system (CMS), are up to the task of handling your content.*

- *It assesses needs for teams, workflow, and management, and it identifies gaps.*

- *It shapes content governance and determines the feasibility of future projects.*

A content audit is a cornerstone of content strategy, which governs content marketing. The aim is to perform a *qualitative* analysis of all the content on a website. In some cases, you need to analyze a network of sites or social media presences—any content for which your organization is responsible. A content audit is often performed in tandem with a content inventory, which is the process of creating a *quantitative* analysis of content.

Step 1: Create a Content Inventory

Create a content inventory by recording all the content on the site into a spreadsheet or a text document by page title or by uniform resource locator (URL). Organize this information in outline form, such as by section heading, followed by subsections and pages. If it's an ecommerce site, these headings and subheadings might be something like this:

Shoes > Women's Shoes > Casual Shoes > Sandals > Dr. Scholl's

A company website's headings would align more closely with this taxonomy:

X Corporation > About Us > Management > John Doe

Content strategist Kristina Halvorson recommends assigning a unique number to each section, subsection, and page, such as 1.0, 1.1. and 1.1.1. This can help tremendously in assigning particular pieces of content to the appropriate site section. Some content strategists also color-code different sections on spreadsheets. It gets down to a matter of personal preference, as well as the size and scale of the audit in question.

It's highly recommended that each section, subsection, or page contains an annotation regarding who owns each piece of content, as well as the type of content: text, image, video, PDF, press release, product page, and so on.

- Is it created in-house?

- If it's created in-house, who created it?

- Is it outsourced (third-party content, really simple syndication [RSS] feeds, blog entries, articles from periodicals)?

- Who's responsible for creating, approving, and publishing each piece?

The resulting document is a content inventory. Now it's time to dig into the quality of the content: the content audit. For each of the following steps, it's helpful to assign a grade or ranking to every page, such as a scale of 1 to 5, with 1 meaning "pretty crappy" and 5 being "rockstar fantastic."

Some practitioners say you can shortcut through certain site pages or sections, arguing that certain pieces or content are evergreen. Although that can certainly be the case, a thorough perusal of every piece of content on every page may surprise you. Elements that you thought were set in stone, or changed sitewide, have a nasty habit of coming up and biting you in the behind. An example might be that page displaying the address of the office your company moved out of five years ago, or the "contact" email address pointing to a long-since-departed employee.

> "So long as you're taking the time to audit the content, it pays to audit all the content."

So long as you're taking the time to audit the content, it pays to audit *all* the content.

Step 2: Determine What Your Content Covers

- What's it about?

- What subjects and topics does content address?

- Are page and section titles, headlines, and subheads promising what's actually delivered in the on-page copy?

- Is there a good balance of content addressing products, services, customer service, and "about us" information?

Step 3: Verify Accuracy and Timeliness

- Is it accurate and up-to-date?

- In a word, is the content topical?

- Are there outdated products or hyperlinks, or is there outdated or inaccurate information lurking in nooks and crannies of the site?

As mentioned, localities, employees, pricing, industry data and statistics, and other information change over time. In addition to checking for factual accuracy, identify content that is outdated as "update/revise" or "remove."

Step 4: Determine Whether Your Content Is Consistent with Your Goals

Does your content support both user and business goals? Many constituencies feed into a company's digital presence: senior management, sales, marketing and PR, customer service—to name but a few. Different divisions may be trying to achieve varying goals in "their" section of a site or blog, but fundamentally all content must gracefully serve two masters: the needs of the business and the needs of the customer. This means, for example, that calls-to-action must be clear, but not so overwhelming that they get in the way of the user experience. The content audit grades content on its ability to achieve both of these goals while staying in balance.

Step 5: Note Whether People Are Finding and Using Your Content

Are people finding and using the content? This is where web analytics comes into play.

- What types of content—and what pages in particular—are the most and least popular on the site in question?

- Where do users spend time, and where do they go when they leave?

- Are users taking desired actions on a page, whether clicking to buy, downloading a whitepaper, or filling out a contact form?

- What search keywords and phrases bring people to the site?

It's not enough that content is simply there. The numbers don't lie. They can reveal what's working, what's not, and direct a strategy that supports more of the types of content users use and seek.

Step 6: Verify Whether the Content Is Clean and Professional

- Is it clean and professional?

- Is page copy consistent in tone?

- Are spellings, punctuation, and grammar consistent and, above all, correct?

- Are abbreviations and acronyms standard?

- If the site has a style guide, is it being followed?

- Are images captioned in a consistent manner and properly placed/oriented on the page?

- Do hyperlinks follow any predesignated rules, such as by opening a new page in a separate browser window?

Step 7: Take Stock of the Content Organization

- Is content logically organized?

- Does the site contain tacked-on pages that don't follow navigational structure?

- Does the overall navigation make sense?

- Are there redundancies, such as on the site shown in Figure 20.1, which lists "Personal Finance" as a separate section in the navigation and then again lists that section in a submenu under the heading "Money & Careers"? This site also lists the same story twice—once with a large photo and stacked head and once with a small photo and a standard headline.

Figure 20.1 *Note the drop-down menu list subsections "careers" and "personal finance." What's the next topline navigation item? Personal Finance. That, friends, is redundant content. Same problem with the lead story, too.*

- Finally, when users visit a section, do they find what they expect to? GreenCine, a Netflix competitor, offers particularly good examples of badly organized content. Take the taxonomy and navigation of the following content sections, for example. Pity the user looking for new DVDs to rent who stumbles on newsletter archives, or the seeker of a back issue of the newsletter who lands on contests and giveaways. Both the naming of links and pages, as well as the navigational structure, are woefully misleading and off-kilter.

Click on the site section "New and Coming Releases" and you land on a page named "New on DVD." What does that page actually contain? Archives of the sites customer newsletter—not exactly what you'd expect.

Meanwhile, the link named Dispatch Newsletter Archives, which you would think would take you to just that, brings the user to a page called "GreenCine PR, Marketing, Events."   Only what's actually on the page are contents and giveaways. Far below the fold, that same page links to the same newsletters archived on the "New on DVD" page.

If you really persevere, you'll finally click on the link labeled New to GreenCine. That's where a user can find actual listings of new/soon-to-be-released DVDs.

Figure 20.2   *Clicking on these links is more likely to take users on a wild goose chase rather than to the section of the site they expect to visit.*

Step 8: Evaluate the Tone of Voice

Every brand, every business has a distinct voice that expresses its personality. Serious, irreverent, scholarly, authoritative; all are valid, but the tone, language, and mode of expression must be a fit and must be consistent with the brand. This step evaluates the content's tendency to spill into multiple personality disorder.

Step 9: Note the Keywords, Metadata, and SEO

- Are target keywords and phrases used on the site and on appropriate pages in the most advantageous places?

- Are page descriptions and metadata used appropriately?

- Are images and multimedia files captioned, and is metadata employed to make them search-engine friendly?

- Are headlines optimized for search?

Search engine optimization begins and ends with content, so evaluating to what extent content conforms to best practices in search is an essential part of an audit.

Step 10: Identify Any Gaps

- What are the weaknesses, gaps, and content needs? Conducting a content audit focuses so much attention on what's there that it's often too easy to overlook what's not there.

- Are issues surrounding shipping and order fulfillment adequately addressed?

- Is the press/media section strong on press releases but weak on photos and video offerings?

- Does the company blog address company issues heavily but general industry trends not at all?

What's missing speaks volumes about the forward direction of a content strategy.

Step 11: Define the Needed Changes/Actions

This is where the rubber hits the road. It's not enough to produce a giant spreadsheet. The goal is to define gaps and problems, as well as identify strengths and develop specific recommendations for improvement.

21

How to Analyze Content Needs

"Knowing you need content is not unlike moving into a new, completely empty house and knowing you need furniture."

We discussed content auditing back in Chapter 20, "How to Conduct a Content Audit." Part of the content auditing process involves performing a gap analysis, a rather fancy-pants way of saying, "Figure out what isn't there, and then figure out how to get it in there."

Easier said than done. Knowing you need content is not unlike moving into a new, completely empty house and knowing you need furniture. Of course, you do. But what kind? What style? What color? What pieces for what rooms? How much do you require to be functional and practical, and how much would make things cluttered and impractical?

Even after you've boiled it down to "sofa for the living room," you still have to decide if it's a sectional, has arms, and you ought to order the matching footrest.

Fortunately, there are systematic ways to go about analyzing and assessing content needs. This includes not only what kind of content is required and in what format, but other factors as well including how often, when, and where to reach which target audience segment effectively.

This might seem painfully obvious to some, but one of the most effective ways to assess content needs is to ask. Interview customers, clients, and prospects about their content needs and their content consumption habits.

Where to Start?

Sources: Ask how these various constituencies consume content and what sources they get content from. Do they subscribe to newsletters? Read blogs? Listen to podcasts? Use search engines when researching a purchase or service? Do they visit company websites, read customer reviews on retail sites, download whitepapers? Do they watch online videos? Follow links on social network sites or Twitter? Do they use their mobile devices or subscribe to RSS feeds? What online publications do they read? Do they participate in online user groups or forums?

It's also helpful to uncover the specifics of these channels. Do they read blogs or not? If they do, which blogs or bloggers do they most avidly follow? What's their favorite publication? Their must-see or must-read sources of digital information? These may or may not lie within your professional sphere; nonetheless, they will help when it comes to assessing taste, style preferences, and predilections.

> "You don't want to create content so infrequently that readers forget about you. But you also don't want to inundate your audience."

How Much, How Often?

We've all been there: subscribed to a newsletter, or eagerly following a cool blog, until suddenly it became too much. Way too much. Creating too much content is an onerous task for you, but it also can quickly sour in the minds of your audience. That eagerly awaited weekly newsletter? When the publisher bumped it up to twice a week instead of once per week, it started looking and feeling more like spam. You don't want to create content so infrequently that readers forget about you. But you also don't want to inundate your audience. It's not impolite to politely inquire as to the frequency of content—and contacts—when assessing content needs.

Part of this assessment is "how much?" For many users, a whitepaper is too long. So is a video on YouTube that runs over five or ten minutes. Some users will want the content equivalent of a snack; others will prefer a five-course meal. Many may want something in between. (And all of this may be contingent on where they are in the consideration and buying cycle.) Scoping out content "serving sizes" is an essential part of a content needs assessment.

When?

Sure, lots of digital content just sits there, waiting for you to find it. A website, a video on YouTube, a whitepaper, a slide show. One of the wonderful things about the Internet is that you can access all these channels in your proverbial pajamas, whenever you want. But for some types of content (not to mention some consumers), it's all in the timing.

Ask when people consume content: at home? At work? Over the weekend? The type of business or service you offer can play a big role in this. Mainframe computers are probably an at-work type of content affair. If you sell pizza or movies or skiing, you may be better off sending that newsletter or tweeting late in the week, perhaps after the workday is done. (Or just before it's time to call it a day.) Common sense dictates that most people would rather be exposed to messaging about coffee in the early morning, beer in the late afternoon. (Yes, there will always be exceptions to those guidelines, but that's why we establish guidelines in the first place.)

Another reason "when" matters is because, although there's plenty of digital content waiting for you to come 'n' get it, increasingly, digital channels are about real-time, or near real-time, messaging. In particular, tweets and posts on social networks such as Facebook, Google+, or LinkedIn are more likely to get readership as well as to be promoted, "liked," amplified, and passed along by readers if they appear at the right time of day, or on the right day of the week.

Interviewing key audience members and members of a target market is only the first step in assessing content needs. Turning to web metrics and other analytics sources is another essential part of the task.

Elements to look for in this arena, both on a website and on external sources such as social media and social network sites, include traffic, comments, "likes," pass-alongs, and other shout-outs. What kinds of content, and in what channels, are attracting the most traffic, attention, recommendations, and chatter in terms of comments and retweets? Conversely, what's dormant and attracts little to no user attention and engagement?

One of the most essential tools in a web analytics package when it comes to assessing and analyzing content needs is search keywords: The words and phrases searchers use to find you on the Web. These terms can help quickly identify user needs. "What toothbrush is best for fighting plaque?" is an example of a search term that reveals a problem the searcher is eager to solve. How can you create content that addresses the problem and that uses those terms, so more searchers with that problem are likely to find your content?

Keyword research reveals the words and phrases searchers use to find you. Combined with the free keyword research tools offered by the major search engines, these words and phrases can be greatly expanded upon. A recent project with a client, for example, was conducting keyword research around the products and merchandise they were targeting at "readers." A quick dig into Google's keyword research tool quickly revealed that searchers don't look for products for "readers," but they do search for items to buy for "book lovers" and even for "bibliophiles."

It's not that people never search the word "readers." (It's important to keep keyword research information in context.) The point is that when searchers are shopping, they're not shopping for "readers." This one nugget of information has made the company's content marketing more effective, influencing the content and even the categories on its blog, the posts on its Facebook page, and even the tweets on Twitter.

Sure, you can always go with your gut when it comes to creating strong content for marketing. But backing up those gut instincts with research, observation, and hard data will always make a content marketing initiative that much more impactful and effective.

22

The Content Workflow

"Get this part right, and you'll be ready to run a newsroom."

Having developed personas, analyzed content needs, developed a content strategy, and appointed someone in a managing editor/editorial lead capacity, the next step in content marketing is to establish a content workflow. This is the point at which content marketing gets tactical. It's the nuts-and-bolts process: content calendars, creation, approvals, style guides, templates, and tools.

Get this part right, and you'll be ready to run a newsroom. And that, after all, is a big part of the concept of content marketing.

At the core of establishing a content workflow is creating an editorial calendar. An editorial calendar establishes what content will be created, when, in what format, and for which content channel. A digital editorial calendar also tracks the *connections* for that content, including how content will be repurposed and amplified in social media channels.

The editorial calendar should contain a list of all content approved for publication. It should address the questions *how much* content, *how often*, and specifically *when* it will publish. It includes content requirements, responsibilities, and a schedule.

The editorial calendar should be governed by a master calendar that takes into account key dates and events. It not only provides an overview of what content will publish by day, week, or month, but also ties that broader schedule together with specifics such as holidays, trade shows, company announcements, events (such as webinars), or new product launches. Don't forget to take international holidays into account if content is targeted to foreign countries. These key dates should also help inform the editorial calendar with ideas for content themed for the Christmas season, perhaps, or a major industry conference at which you'll be releasing a whitepaper.

> "You know you have to create something, but you don't have a clue what that something should be."

The editorial calendar also serves as an invaluable map for repurposing content. Say you're publishing a whitepaper or research report. How and when will that information be broken down and funneled into other channels such as your blog, a press release, or an update on a social network such as Facebook, Twitter, LinkedIn, or Google+? It should also act as a reminder to collect appropriate graphic elements such as photos, charts or graphs, or multimedia content, to enhance the written word.

The editorial calendar should funnel "real-world" content into digital channels. Perhaps an executive is speaking at a conference or has made a media appearance. Capture that presentation and share it on SlideShare or YouTube.

Having those holiday reminders in the calendar should be taken seriously, and they should be leavened with common sense. Seasoned editors don't publish their best material late on a Friday afternoon in summer when their target audience is beach-bound, just as a financial services company should hold back publishing on a bank holiday Monday. That's just common sense; you want your content to have the maximum possible impact.

Editorial calendars track what kind of content is created, when it's created, and how often. For example, your calendar might show that you post twice daily to Twitter, blog three times a week, and send out newsletters twice per month, on Wednesdays.

Editorial calendars are also critical tools in tracking ideas for content and what types of content are to be created. For example, a company striving to post four times per week on its blog might shoot for one originally authored piece, one commentary on current industry news, one guest post from an outside expert, and one round-up of curated links on interesting topics related to the business. Having specific goals helps to alleviate that "white page" syndrome when you know you have to create *something*, but you don't have a clue what that something should be.

Many editorial calendars also incorporate the production process into the mix, which is a great way to ensure content creation is on track. This can include who's responsible for individual content elements, when a first draft is due, who conducts the copy edit, and when (often, with a specific time) the final draft will be received and proofed, entered into the CMS (or newsletter template, or blog platform) system, and pushed live, or published.

A follow-up to that can be outlining a process for promoting and disseminating the content on social media: tweeting, linking to, and otherwise amplifying the content. Whose job is that, and when will they do it? The editorial calendar should address this aspect of connect-the-dots content.

More Tools of the Trade

The editorial calendar is a must-have tool for any content marketing strategy, and one that can be adapted to varying needs. What follows is a list of additional resources for the content "newsroom" that range from nice-to-have to must-have elements of content marketing initiatives, depending on the organization and goals.

- **Personas**—Discussed at length in Chapter 8, "Content Curation and Aggregation," the archetype characters represent the varying segments of a target audience.

- **Keyword List**—Based on search engine optimization (SEO) research, this is the list of words and phrases most critical to your business, products, and services when it comes to being found on the Web. If you don't have an SEO expert on staff, anyone and everyone involved in content creation should receive foundational training in SEO and how to appropriately use keywords (and other SEO principles) in content creation.

- **Brand Brief**—Most organizations with a marketing department have already created this (usually one-page-long) description of the corporate brand.

- **Style Guide (Writing)**—A detailed and comprehensive set of rules and guidelines for written content (see Figure 22.1). Very often, the grammar and usage portion of this guide is based on an existing, standard source such as the *AP Stylebook*, and it's adapted for the organization's content needs (see Figure 22.2). This document should also address tone, voice, and writing style. Very often, it addresses web elements; for example, when a link is embedded in text, does it open a new page or redirect the user entirely?

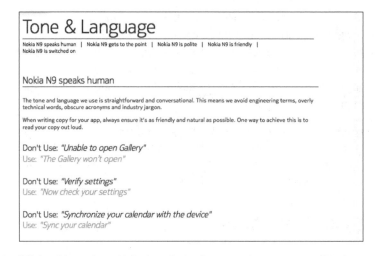

Figure 22.1   *Notice how Nokia's style guide encourages writing with a human, rather than a technical, tone of voice to make communications warmer and more understandable. Providing examples such as these is always a great idea in a style guide, rather than broader abstractions that are open to misinterpretation.*

Figure 22.2   *The AP Stylebook, a standard building block of style guides in journalism as well as in the business world.*

- **Style Guide (Design)**—The visual counterpart to the writing style guide that's a comprehensive set of rules and guidelines for visual design. It should outline proper usage (and, when necessary, how to attribute credit) for photos, images, embedded videos, fonts, and color schemes. Issues this document should address include, for example, whether an image posted to the blog should be justified right, left, or center. How much whitespace should surround it, top and bottom? Do all images require captions?

- **Editing Guidelines**—A checklist to ensure that editors (and in many cases, copy editors) are thorough to ensure high-quality content. It's the editors' job to uphold all the style guide requirements, of course. They are also responsible for checking facts, ascertaining that submitted content is original, validating hyperlinks, proofing images to ensure they're properly labeled and tagged, and a variety of other critical housekeeping tasks.

- **Graphics Repository**—A collection of ready-to-use images such as logos, executive portraits, and product shots that the content team can easily find and deploy. Depending on needs, you may also want to make multimedia material available in the manner.

- **Submission Brief**—An outline of expectations and concepts (often accompanied by a visual template) for outside or occasional content contributors. You'll be glad you have this once you've explained, in detail, how to submit an article to your blog or your newsletter for the twelfth consecutive time!

- **Maintenance Plan**—Can be either a calendar or more general scheduling guidelines for removing or archiving outdated content, as well as assigning that responsibility to someone on the team.

23

Listening...And Responding

Listen up!

If you think content marketing is only about content creation and publication, think again. Listening online is the foundation of any content marketing initiative.

Without listening to relevant online conversations, news, blogs, influencers, and other online content, you cannot possibly craft an effective content marketing strategy, nor can you tactically advance the execution forward, refining as you go. At the heart of content marketing is listening, responding, and crafting appropriate content based on what's "out there."

Lather, rinse, repeat. Always be listening! Author and digital marketing consultant Chris Brogan recommends the following ratio when it comes to online content creation: 25% listening, 50% commenting/responding, and 25% publishing.

Why Listen?

Establishing and constantly monitoring a well-conceived list of places and people online serves a variety of critical needs. It's a way to stay plugged in to the wants, needs, concerns, complaints, and behaviors of both customers and prospects. It's a way to stay attuned to their sentiments toward your company and its products and services—as well as those of competitors. In addition to keeping you on top of general trends in the news and industry, it's insight into target markets. What excites them? Angers them? Engages them?

> "It's a big Internet out there. No one can possibly listen to everything, so it's essential to establish goals."

This information serves a variety of purposes, including these:

- It shapes the types of content you create, as well as the channels it's distributed on.

- It rapidly addresses complaints and customer service gripes, often enabling snuffing out a smoldering flame before it erupts into a wildfire.

- Via listening, you can identify the top influencers in your field, the ones whose help and support you'll want to enlist in publicizing or advocating your messages. Without listening, even if you know who those people are, you won't be equipped to properly engage with them.

It's a big Internet out there. No one can possibly listen to everything, so it's essential to establish goals to effectively listen, not to mention turning learning into action.

Broadly put, the main objectives of listening can be one or more of the following:

- **Thought leadership**—Monitor discussion around key industry issues and trends to join the conversation to establish credibility and innovative thought around your brand, company, or executives.

- **Content and product development**—Listening to expressed needs, then meeting that demand. This can be applied to products (automotive manufacturers have applied online listening to refining and designing new cars), or even content and intellectual capital generated by your organization (people seem interested in our product, but they'd be more inclined to buy if they realized how much money it would save them over five years.)

- **Brand/product sentiment**—Listening can provide alerts in near-real time when a company, its products, or services are mentioned online either positively or negatively.

- **Customer service**—Countless companies have connected and empowered their customer support teams with a variety of social media channels to deal with complaints and people in need of customer support. Listening to customer support issues is also invaluable in creating online help centers, customer forums, product documentation, and other forms of content that enable customers to help themselves (which can radically lower customer support and call center costs).

What to Listen For

Developing a list of what conversations, keywords, and terms to listen for is core to any listening strategy and loops back into the goals of a listening campaign. The list should be prioritized so focus can be directed where it's needed. Some of the most obvious things to follow are listed here, but marketers have to make their own choices and then adjust those choices continually for reasons ranging from seasonality (a Thanksgiving promotion, for example) to new keywords and phrases and products being added or removed from the listening campaign.

Following are some of the most obvious things you should be listening for:

- Name of company
- Name(s) of product(s)
- Names of top executives
- Industry/Product keywords: talk around your area of specialization ("mountain climbing boots" "adjustable rate mortgage"), competitor-related names, terms, and phrases.
- Seasonal keywords
- Local keywords, such as "brand name + chicago"

How and Where to Listen

After determining what to listen for, deciding where to listen is the next most critical step in monitoring online content and conversations. An entire industry of sophisticated social media monitoring and listening software has grown up around this. Commercially available software packages now offer all sorts of ways to listen, as well as algorithms that automatically monitor and weigh whether chatter, articles, and blog posts (to name a few) are more postive or negative and how they reflect overall brand sentiment.

It's not always necessary to invest in expensive, highly technical solutions when it comes to listening. There are a few basic—and free—tools anyone can set up to listen to digital news and chatter. Google Alerts (shown in Figure 23.1) is a good example of a free tool you can use.

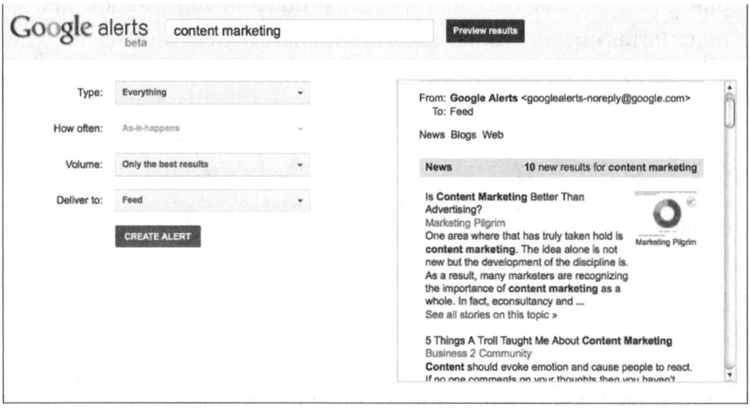

Figure 23.1   Google Alerts is one of the most fundamental and valuable online listening tools out there. Best of all, it's free.

After listening keywords and phrases have been established, set them up and track them in Google Alerts. It will notify you, via email or RSS feed (your choice), when selected terms appear on the open Web. Needless to say, Google Alerts can't go where Google's searchbots aren't welcome. Private discussion forums and user groups, or protected Facebook pages, are just a couple obvious examples of the limits of this still-indispensable tool.

There are many reasons why a marketer would parse listening campaigns into segments. What's discussed in the news, for example, can differ from or influence the chatter in the blogsphere or on Twitter. Often, it's useful, if not critical, to the success of a listening campaign to slice and dice monitoring into channel segments.

Fortunately, this is easy to do, and there's no shortage of free tools to help accomplish the task at hand. All the major news portals (Yahoo's is pictured in Figure 23.2) allow users to set up alerts for breaking news stories.

Similarly, you can configure blog search tools such as Technorati and Google Blog search to send alerts when there are mentions in the blogosphere.

Twitter has its own search engine. You can use it to find specific words and phrases, but it's also helpful for following hashtags, those subject matter labels preceded by the hash sign (#), such as #contentmarketing (see Figure 23.3). In addition to Twitter's search engine, a variety of free, third-party tools for Twitter (TweetDeck is probably the most popular) can easily be configured to search for and follow conversations around a variety of parameters, specific users (real names or Twitter handles), keyword terms, or hashtags, just for starters.

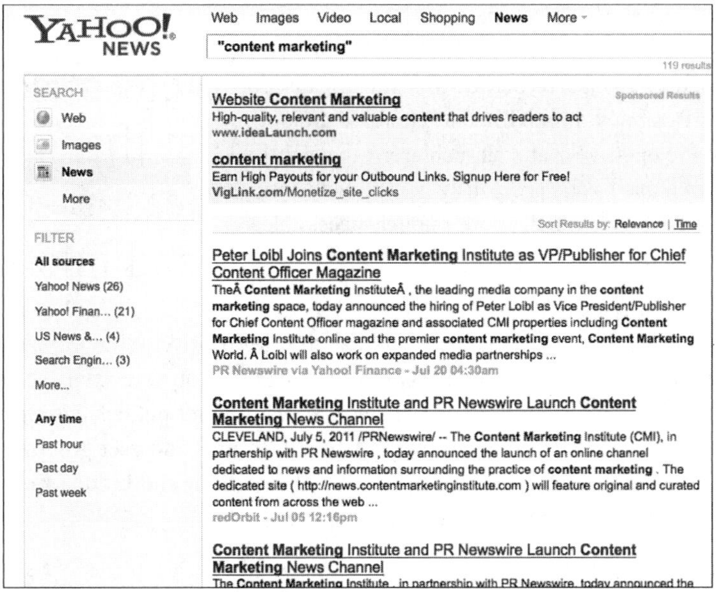

Figure 23.2   *It's easy to set up free breaking news alerts on Yahoo, Google, or any other major news portal.*

Figure 23.3   *Twitter can easily be searched, in real time, for keywords, phrases, people, and hashtags.*

Other channels that are necessary to monitor may not be so straightforward. Online discussion boards, forums, user groups, or private or semi-private profiles on Facebook, LinkedIn, and Google+ are not part of the open Web and as such aren't crawlable and searchable by the previously mentioned tools and channels that are all about publicly accessible information.

> "Forewarned is forearmed...or at the very least prepared and informed."

Listening in these channels can require considerably more legwork and a more hands-on approach. It's a relatively straightforward matter to monitor, for example, comments and posts made on your own Facebook page, but digging deeper into what may be relevant, if not publicly visible conversations, often requires joining and participating in forums and user groups and creating online social connections with subject matter experts and influencers in distinct circles of conversation and spheres of influence.

Why does it matter if such talk is private, anyway? Issues people are passionate about often bubble to the surface. Forewarned is forearmed...or at the very least prepared and informed. Listening prepares you not only to create and disseminate outbound messaging and content, but also to deal appropriately with inbound comments, messages, criticism, and yes, even hostility. You'll know the players, the community, and its rules of engagement before being sideswiped by discussions that come as a complete surprise and for which you're unprepared, or unequipped, to deal with.

Involve Others and Assign Roles

Much of the information collected by listening in digital channels will help shape content marketing strategy and messaging moving forward. Other comments, queries, and complaints demand an instant response team. This necessitates creating a system for disseminating listening data and creating a team of people tapped with providing responses, often in near-real time.

To achieve this, a number of questions must be addressed regarding the team charged with addressing social chatter. This may be a team of one, for smaller organizations, or of dozens or hundreds of people, as is often the case today in large corporations.

Questions to address include how team members are notified that their help or input (such as subject matter expertise) is needed. Email? Instant message (IM)? A dashboard? How quickly will members be notified, and is there a window or deadline for providing a response? Is the response to be vetted and approved, or do team members have the authority to respond directly?

Equally important, who responds? Does a single name, face, or avatar represent the entire organization, or do different people (Joe in Sales, Sue in Customer Care, for example) respond to different queries and complaints?

Finally, what's the follow-up procedure for recording interactions and determining how they can be folded into ongoing content marketing initiatives? When questions, queries, and complaints are flowing in regarding one specific product feature, for example, there's a pretty strong signal that more informative content is needed around that product or feature.

Without this sort of careful planning and assessment, you risk alienating users and their communities, as well as fanning flames of anger into a bonfire of ill will, as happened to Nestlé (see Figure 23.4).

Figure 23.4   *When the company failed to respond appropriately to users' environmental concerns around Nestlé, the company's Facebook page erupted into a virulent hatefest.*

Responding

A social listening plan is not just about dealing with angry customers, but it will help enormously in dealing with and quelling online complaints before they mushroom. Often, responding and demonstrating that you're paying attention and want to set things right is response enough (and something users are beginning to expect). Negative comments can be turned into positive experiences. Moreover, social tools help determine the influence and scope of those comments and can be factored into the type of response delivered. Someone on Facebook or Twitter with thousands of followers wields considerable influence when they compliment or complain about a company or its products.

Carefully crafted responses should always be delivered in the channels from whence they came. Twitter conversations stay in Twitter, and Facebook remains on Facebook. Sometimes (particularly on Twitter) it's difficult to respond effectively in 140 characters or less. Still, this is the channel in which an appropriate response might involve inviting the commenter into a longer conversation, perhaps via email. And always, always pay attention to the wake of an online conversation; don't simply respond and walk away.

As with any other form of content marketing, responding is very much about being helpful and building relationships, not about being sales-y. By monitoring discussions about the best type of product to buy, for example, by all means contribute to the discussion. Disclose your interest of affiliation with your product. But don't go posting links and banners and buy-mes. Your role is to help and become a trusted authority, not a shill or the digital equivalent of a used car salesman.

By behaving responsibly and with authority in the context of a given community, you'll not only build relationships with influencers but hopefully, given time, become one yourself.

24

Remaking, Remodeling, and Repurposing Content

"Every marketer with half a brain knows viral isn't something you can buy in a bottle."

Everyone knows glass is recyclable. Until recently, no one realized just how far glass recycling could go in a digital environment. A video made for a Corning investor event in early 2011 has (much to the surprise of Corning executives and its agency) gone mega-viral on YouTube. With upward of eight million views in four short weeks, it's the most-watched corporate video in YouTube history. Maybe even in all of corporate video history.

Every marketer with half a brain knows viral isn't something you can buy in a bottle. And if it were, it wouldn't come with a guarantee. But what smart marketers who invest time and dollars into content creation do know is that reusing and recycling that content can far extend the reach of their message and the return on investment (ROI) of their spend.

Take Sony's breathtaking, award-winning Bravia ads from circa 2006–2007. Users and fans—not Sony or its agency—uploaded them to YouTube where they live in perpetuity, garnering *in toto* some five million views.

Small wonder advertisers got in on the action. Chrysler's ad from the 2011 Super Bowl has enjoyed more than nine million views on the company's YouTube channel, extending reach and justifying some of that enormous spend on creative.

Yet recycling content is hardly reserved for the big boys. Small businesses, mom 'n' pops, and even individuals polishing their personal brands online are learning that if content marketing counts, extending the life and the reach of that content makes it count oh, so much more.

Simple, right? Only too few marketers make content recycling part of a content marketing strategy.

Slice 'n' Dice

The Internet runs on content and offers seemingly endless distribution options for all kinds of media: text, images, video, audio, you name it. Yet content creation can be hard. It requires thought. Ideas. Strategy. Data. Production. Editing. Originality. Relevance. Targeting.

> "Creative is hard. Recycling is relatively easy."

After you've produced a strong piece of content, the goal should be to leverage it in different channels, different formats, and different media for maximum impact. Creative is hard. Recycling is relatively easy—and increasing reach is nothing to sneeze at.

For example, say you (or a company executive) are speaking at an industry event. The speech? New content. That's a lotta work. But look at it this way: In the run-up to the event, it lightens the load in other areas. You can blog and tweet about the upcoming talk. Not just promote it, mind you, but drip out tantalizing bits of information and perhaps data or finding that will encourage attendance.

Now that the speech is done and delivered, you did remember to do a video of its delivery, didn't you? In whole or in parts, the speech can go on your site, your blog, YouTube, you name it. Perhaps the audio is appropriate for a podcast. Transcribe the presentation both to boost SEO rankings of the audio and video and perhaps as a stand-alone text marketing piece. (Email newsletter, anyone?)

The presentation itself? Up onto Slideshare it goes. Extract charts, infographics, and other nuggets of easy-to-digest visual data to build short-burst content around.

Can the talk be turned into—or incorporated into—a whitepaper? An ebook? Is there something newsworthy in it that's press-releasable? Perhaps it's webinar material, with just the right amount of tweaking.

Note this approach doesn't just apply to a one-off event such as a speech. When a content marketing editorial calendar is mapped, part of the process is to determine how to tweet each blog post, and once a post goes up, how to recycle its essence into other content marketing channels such as articles, videos, and newsletters.

As You Listen, So Shall You Create Content

Customers and prospects are likely shoving all kinds of content in your direction. You could use it—if only you were listening.

What questions and topics of discussion arise most frequently in user forums and in discussion around your brand—or product category—in social media channels? Taking a cue from consumer issues, questions, and resolutions enables you to create how-to content, useful FAQs, and user manuals. Listening could even result in content that funnels in to product development.

It's Doubtful You'll Be Repeating Yourself

Post-Thanksgiving eating is an analogy that could apply to content recycling. There's roast turkey on the big day, followed by turkey hash, turkey sandwiches, and cold turkey sliced in salad. Perhaps someone whips up a pot of turkey chili. When you're eating at home, all that turkey is likely feeding the same audience.

That's not necessarily so with content. In fact, it's unlikely. Your own analytics will bear this out, but it's improbable there's terribly significant overlap between your newsletter subscribers, Facebook and Twitter followers, and the people who read your blog. Different segments have different content appetites: the form, the length, the medium, and the channel. And in case you haven't noticed, there's a lot of content out there. Brand impressions and engagement count.

So do learnings about format, channels, style, and the relative length or brevity of your content. Recycling not only frees you from the burden of being a virtual new-idea factory, it's also a sandbox in which you can experiment with what's working—and with whom.

25

Tools of the Trade

*There are lots and lots and **lots** of tools out there to help with nearly every aspect of content marketing, from setting up sites to managing images, text, and graphics; measuring success; listening and responding; and so much more.*

The list that follows is by no means comprehensive. Instead, it focuses on many of the leading and (mostly) free tools available to marketers that will aid in their content marketing efforts.

Don't get overwhelmed. Instead, view this list as a starting point to explore what's out there. No one will need or want to use every tool on this list. Some will become essential to your content marketing campaigns, whereas others you can ignore completely. No one, but no one, needs 20 different Twitter analytics solutions—but they're out there. Also note that as the Web in general, and social media in particular, evolves, many of these tools can be hard to categorize. Many actually fit into several categories and serve multiple purposes.

By exploring what's available and playing around with some of the tools on the following lists, however, you'll doubtless discover a tool or two that will make content marketing initiatives better, faster, more relevant, or more accountable.

So dig in, and have fun.

Social Networks

- **Facebook**—World's largest social network. Individual, company, product, and cause pages.

- **LinkedIn**—Business-oriented social network. Individual and company profiles.

- **Twitter**—Microblogging social network. Posts limited to 140 characters.

- **Google+**—The new kid on the block. Create "circles" of different target audiences for posts.

- **Ning**—Create your own social network.

- **Foursquare**—Hyperlocal social network based on location check-ins.

- **Gowalla**—A Foursquare alternative.

Listening Tools

- **Google Alerts**—Set up alerts for keywords and phrases that are automatically delivered via email or RSS feeds.

- **Yahoo! Groups**—There are interest and discussion groups around nearly every topic. Listen, and participate in conversations to assess trends, interests, and sentiment.

- **Google Groups**—See above: Google's alternative service to Yahoo! Groups, though using one service should not preclude the other.

- **Google Reader**—One of the best RSS readers.

- **Backtype**—Follow and share comments on the Web.

- **Social Mention**—Real-time social media search results.

- **Boardreader**—Monitors top public online forums.

- **wikiAlarm**—Alerts when a Wikipedia entry has been changed.

- **Tinker**—Discover conversations on Facebook and Twitter.

- **Surchur**—Real-time social media search and discovery.

- **Quora Online**—Knowledge hub for question and answer exchanges.

- **Addict-o-matic**—Create a custom page to display search and buzz results.

- **MonitorThis**—Subscribe to up to 20 really simple syndication (RSS) feeds through one stream.

- **Blogpulse**—Analyzes and reports on daily trends in the blogosphere.

- **Commentful**—Watches comments/follow-ups on blog posts and other social media content.

- **HowSociable?**—Brand visibility on the social web.

- **Samepoint**—Reputation management search engine.

- **Keotag**—Search for tags on blogs, search engines, and social bookmarking sites from one location.

- **LinkedIn Answers**—LinkedIn members can pose business relation questions and receive answers. A great showcase for knowledge and expertise.

- **LinkedIn Groups**—Much like Yahoo! or Google Groups, LinkedIn's version is business-oriented.

- **Yahoo! Answers**—Like LikedIn's offering but open to the general pubic, so questions (and answers) apply to every conceivable topic.

Twitter Management

- **TweetDeck**—Highly customizable Twitter management system.

- **HootSuite**—Manage multiple accounts from one dashboard.

- **Twitterfeed**—Set RSS feeds to automatically post on Twitter.

- **Twitter Search**—Search Twitter in real time. For tagging, use the # (hash) tag.

- **Tweetmeme**—What's hot on Twitter.

- **Twilert**—Emails Twitter search alerts.

- **Yammer**—A Twitter-like application for enterprise.

- **Tagalus**—Directory of Twitter hash tags.

- **MyTweeple**—Manage tweets and followers, including multiple profiles.

- **Twitter Facebook App**—Update Facebook via Twitter.

- **Selective Twitter Facebook App**—Update Facebook only when you use #fb.

- **Seesmic**—Manage multiple Twitter accounts.

- **CoTweet**—Twitter customer relationship management (CRM) tool.

Twitter Analytics and Measurement

- **TweetStats**—Charts Twitter frequency, who you retweet and reply to most, when you tweet most, and so on.

- **Twitter Analyzer**—Graphs data such as tweet frequency, retweets, tweet count, readers, and more on a graph.

- **Tweet Effect**—Tracks when you lose or gain followers.

- **Twitter Grader**—Checks the power of your Twitter profile compared to millions of other users.

- **Tweet Rush**—Usage stats, including how long, when, and how often you tweet over a given period of time.

- **Tweet Reach**—How many impressions tweets are in a specific timeframe.

- **Twitlyzer**—Calculates influence, quality, and velocity of tweets. Compare stats with other users and generate charts.

- **Twitaholic**—Tracks most popular users.

- **Twitter Grader**—Measures relative influence.

- **TwitterScore**—Another relative ranking tool.

Content Sharing

- **Delicious**—Shared content via social bookmarking.

- **Digg**—News content sharing.

- **Reddit** User-generated news links.

- **Slideshare**—Share PowerPoint presentations.

- **StumbleUpon**—Randomly generates content for users by interest area.

- **YouTube**—The leading video sharing site, owned by Google.

- **Vimeo**—A YouTube alternative.

- **Google Custom Search**—Create a niche search engine for a website or blog.

- **Scribd**—Share original writing.

- **Flickr**—Share/upload/find photos.

- **Picasa**—A Google-owned Flickr alternative.

- **Trunk.ly**—Keeps a history of the links that you like or tweet and makes them searchable and easy to share.

- **Storify**—Aggregate and curate content from around the Web.

PR

- **Marketwire**—Online press release distribution, social media releases, social media monitoring, online newsrooms.

- **PR Newswire**—Press release distribution, targeting, monitoring, and measurement.

- **PRWeb**—Distribute content via traditional and social media news releases.

- **PitchEngine**—Create and send social media releases to networks, and personalize them with images, videos, bullet points, and graphics.

Blogging

There are too many blog platforms to mention. Recommended, not just for blogging but also as content management systems fully capable of supporting a full website, are **WordPress**, **TypePad** and **Drupal**. The best "lightweight" platforms that are highly customizable, support multimedia content, and are easy to post to (for example, via email) are **Tumblr** and **Posterous**.

- **Technorati**—Blog directory and search engine.

- **IceRocket**—Search for blogs and blog posts by category.

- **Google Blog Search**—Blog search engine.

- **Zemanta**—Easily add additional content and links to blog posts.

- **Tipjoy**—Simple social media payment system.

- **Apture**—Search and explore rich content and media from the Web without leaving the page.

- **OnlyWire**—Build back links to a website or blog by submitting posts to 42 social network sites, including Digg, Reddit, and StumbleUpon.

Measurement and Analytics

For Twitter measurement tools, see that section.

- **Google Analytics**—A free and robust web analytics tool.

- **Klout**—Measures overall social media influence.

- **Website Grader**—Free tools from Hubspot that grade a site on analytics and social media indicators.

- **Alexa**—Website traffic information.

- **Compete.com**—Site analytics comparison tool.

- **Quantcast**—Analytics and site demographics.

- **Woopra**—Real-time web analytics, live chat, and statistics, including tracking conversion and funnel reports.

- **Sysomos**—Monitor social media conversations on Twitter, Facebook, LinkedIn, forums and blogs.

- **Facebook Insights**—Provides Facebook Page owners and Facebook Platform developers with metrics around content.

- **Fourscore.it**—Foursquare analytics.

Online Surveys

- **SurveyMonkey**—Create and publish online surveys, and view results graphically and in real time.

- **ClickTools**—Enterprise survey tool with CRM features.

Audio/Video & Graphics

Note: The most popular photo and video sharing sites are in the Content Sharing section.

- **Cinchcast**—Create, broadcast, and analyze audio content from any phone or web-enabled device.

- **Screenr**—Web-based screen recorder.

- **DailyBooth**—Create a photo diary.

- **Skitch**—Fast screen capture, editing, and sharing.

- **Instagram**—Fast, easy iPhone photo sharing.

- **Blinkplan**—Create magazine pagination online.

- **Visual.ly**—Collection of infographics and data visualizations.

- **Gimp**—Image editor.

- **Jimp**—Capture and share anything on your computer screen.

Keyword Research

- **Google AdWords Keyword Tool**—Displays other keywords related to a term you enter. Keywords can be sorted by search volume popularity.

- **Google Trends**—Provides insights into broad search patterns. http://www.google.com/trends

- **Google Insights for Search**—Compares search volume patterns across specific regions, categories, and time frames.

- **Microsoft adCenter**—Keyword research tool affiliated with Microsoft's Bing search engine.

- **Wordtracker Free Keyword Suggestion Tool**—Enter a term, and this tool returns 100 terms related to (and including) the original query, ranked by daily popularity. Data is based on search term data collected from the Dogpile and Metacrawler meta search engines.

- **Trellian Free Search Term Suggestion Tool**—Similar to Wordtracker (previous bullet). Terms are ranked by how often they're searched for annually rather than daily.

- **SEO Book Keyword Suggestion Tool**—Taps into Yahoo's tool and provides links and information regarding many of the preceding tools.

- **Hubspot**—Tracks performance of keywords and competitors' keywords.

Webinar Providers

To run a webinar, you'll need a software platform. The following are the three major providers.

- **GoToMeeting**
- **WebEx**
- **GoToWebinar**

Miscellaneous

Finally, these essential tools for the content marketer defy categorization:

- **Email Marketing Provider**—There are too many to list, but it's more than likely you'll need one to manage email campaigns, newsletters, and address lists. The most reputable email marketing firms are members of the Email Sender and Provider Coalition (www.espcoalition.org).

- **URL Shortener**—To keep uniform resource locators (URLs) in Twitter, post under the 140-character limit. Try goo.gl, bit.ly, or tinyurl.com.

- **AP Stylebook**—Available online, and a great basis from which to build your own customized style guide.

- **Kampyle**—Feedback forms and feedback managment tools for websites and blogs.

- **Bazaarvoice**—Provides customer reviews and user-generated content to ecommerce sites.

26

Yes, But Is It Working? Content Metrics and Analytics

In digital channels, everything can be measured, and content marketing initiatives are no exception to that rule. Without measurement, there's no way of knowing what's working and what isn't. You won't have information upon which you can refine or improve results or jettison the stuff that's less effective.

In short, you should never begin content marketing until you have an ongoing plan for measurement and analysis. Not only will it continually inform endeavors as they move forward, but it also will help justify the time, energy, resources, and budget required to get those endeavors underway to the people in the corner office.

Establish a Measurement Plan

The first step is determining what will be measured. Sounds simple, right? It's not. When you can measure practically everything, narrowing that list to the essentials is a daunting—but necessary task. Skip it, and you put yourself at high risk for what web analytics professionals call "analysis paralysis." Confronted with mountains of web analytics data throws even the most stalwart people into deer-in-headlights mode.

So the first step in setting up a plan for measurement is establishing key performance indicators (KPIs), perhaps five or so. These are the core goals that are foundational to success. KPIs will vary depending on goals. Examples might be newsletter sign-ups, whitepaper downloads, leads from a contact form, increased site traffic, higher search rankings, inbound phone calls, increased online orders, higher brand (or product) awareness, more inbound links, and keyword value. It's your call, so long as KPIs are relevant to business and marketing goals *and* are measurable.

Here's where many a content marketer begins to feel a migraine coming on. Fasten your seatbelt, because math and numbers are necessarily part of this process.

Each KPI should have a dollar value assigned to it. (In desperate situations where dollars really don't cut it, use a point system.) Dollars are better because they reflect real business goals and situations. As an example, if your sales team can close one $300 sale per 10 leads generated by a contact form, you know each lead is worth $30.

An excellent example of assigning value to content comes from the BrainTraffic blog—a content strategy agency based in Minneapolis. It outlined how to assign value to a website that sells furniture:

- The average chair costs $500.

- Analytics show 50 people start the process of purchasing a chair online every day, but only 10 finish the process.

- User research shows the instructions on the purchase pages to be confusing.

- We assume 5–10 people leave the purchasing process because of something unrelated to the site, and 5–10 leave the process when they see the shipping costs.

- We assume the remaining 20–30 people would complete the purchasing process if the instructions were more helpful.

- Therefore, the value of the instructional content is likely around $300,000–$450,000 per month ($500 × 20–30 people × 30 days).

- The cost of fixing the content is approximately $25,000.

How's that for proving the value of content? Bear in mind that you are certainly allowed to periodically review and amend KPIs, as well as establish new ones for new projects.

Measure early, often, and at regular intervals. And don't forget to set aside a budget for measurement. Although many measurement tools are low-cost, if not free (many of which are listed in the next section), measuring and analysis places strong demands on time and resources.

Bear in mind that standard web analytics packages aren't the only tools in the measurement arsenal. There's a dizzying array of software out there that monitors Facebook, Twitter, and the blogosphere; benchmarks your site against your competitors'; or enables you to run surveys and polls. Choose your tools wisely.

An Example of Business-to-Business Content Marketing Measurement

Eloqua's Joe Chernov (you met him in Chapter 19, "Whose Job Is Content?") tracks the leads that the company's content generates on a quarterly basis and keeps an eye on search results every day. He claims the company has closed $2.5 million in annual contracts from clients who downloaded a series of guides published in 2010, with more than $3 million in the contract stage from that same cohort.

Chernov has also demonstrated that people who discover the company through its content are 21% more likely to view a product demonstration. He's also able to demonstrate that these visitors are more likely to be VP level or higher than the average site visitor.

An Example of Business-to-Consumer Content Marketing Measurement

Metrics are considerably different at PepsiCo, one of the country's largest consumer brands. For Shiv Singh, who heads digital, it's all about brand metrics and what consumers say online. Pepsi's Refresh Project awards grants to community service projects nominated by and voted on by consumers. The project began with a four-week virtual focus group on Facebook, after which Pepsi conducted demographic and geographic analysis on 120,000 submitted ideas. This was followed by monitoring the Web for mentions of the project and assessing sentiment.

"The premise behind it is that what consumers say about us is more important than anything that we say," said Singh in an interview with eMarketer. "It's an indexed competitive score looking at how our brand is doing compared to our competitors, indexed on a hundredth scale. The formula accounts for volume and sentiment, and then weighted by platform."

Clearly, Pepsi's KPIs are vastly different from Eloqua's. Selling soft drinks to consumers is vastly different from selling a software solution to businesses. In aggregate, however, the following chart illustrates what corporate marketers from across the spectrum say their content marketing success criteria are.

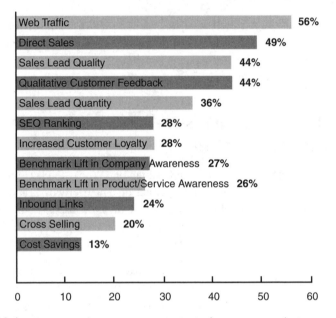

Measurement Criteria for Content Marketing Success

- Web Traffic — 56%
- Direct Sales — 49%
- Sales Lead Quality — 44%
- Qualitative Customer Feedback — 44%
- Sales Lead Quantity — 36%
- SEO Ranking — 28%
- Increased Customer Loyalty — 28%
- Benchmark Lift in Company Awareness — 27%
- Benchmark Lift in Product/Service Awareness — 26%
- Inbound Links — 24%
- Cross Selling — 20%
- Cost Savings — 13%

Figure 26.1   *Most popular measurement criteria for content marketing success by corporate marketers. Source: The Content Marketing Institute*

Although it's always helpful to have this sort of benchmark information, it's important to point out that for the majority of marketers, a much finer point must be put on goals than is evident in this chart. Like a Russian matryoshka doll, most of these broad goals can be broken down into smaller and smaller units of things to measure.

Let's consider the top priorities.

Web Traffic and Engagement

We've evolved well beyond the early Internet era when "clicks" or "hits" were the ultimate goal of a site owner. It's not just traffic that counts. It's what the traffic does that matters: users exhibiting desired behaviors, such as downloading, sharing, commenting, signing up for a newsletter, or calling a call center. Use an analytics package to track behaviors (Goals in Google Analytics) to answer these questions.

Where the traffic goes is equally important. When users consume a piece of content, do they stick with it to the end, or do they bail off the page after only a few seconds? Are they visiting the pages or site sections you want them to?

Others use website analysis to assess that elusive (but oh, so desirable) goal of user engagement. To measure engagement, you have to define it (which no one really has). That's not stopping you from developing a working definition of your own. Perhaps it's someone who viewed three or more pages or spent three or more minutes on the site, or it's a visitor who returned multiple times. Traffic is a metric that can also be applied to social media, such as "likes" on Facebook.

Search keywords are another value that can be effectively tied to traffic. What keywords are visitors using to find your content? What are the highest-converting keywords—the ones that lead visitors where you want them to go or that make them stick around longer and consume more? (You ought to create more content for them!) Keywords are worthwhile for almost any content marketer to measure.

Bottom line? Slice traffic measurement any way you want to, as long as what you measure is consistent, predefined units.

Sales

The only thing that's surprising about sales being marketers' #2 content goal is that it isn't #1. In fact, a survey conducted in 2010 by Bazaarvoice and the CMO Club shows CMOs aspire to move beyond engagement (number of fans, site traffic, and so on) to tie social media more closely into hard business metrics such as revenue and conversion.

Sometimes, as with the furniture site example at the beginning of this chapter, it will be easy to tie content directly into sales. Frequently, as is the case with companies such as Eloqua, no matter how effective the content, there are secondary and often tertiary steps in the sales cycle (most often, long- or short-term cycles of lead generation and consideration).

This is where it's important to build attribution methods into content marketing initiatives to get credit where it's due. Eloqua does this with online forms. Other companies assign discrete 800 numbers to different pieces of content to learn what's generating calls. In some cases, definitively demonstrating that content marketing shortens a sales cycle can be an effective proof of its worth.

> "The only thing that's surprising about sales being marketers' #2 content goal is that it isn't #1."

Qualitative Customer Feedback

Friends, fans, likes, comments, reviews, survey responses—everyone likes to be liked, and being liked does indeed impart value. The question, of course, is how *much* value? A "like" on Facebook from a member with a closed profile or with only a dozen network friends is clearly not worth the same "like" from a member with an open profile…and thousands of friends who see that message.

Feedback serves other purposes than the network effect. Comments on content, product reviews, and tweets can lead to improvements and refinements in products, customer service, and research and development. Recommendations and becoming a fan can aid in branding and awareness or in perception of your company or its executives as credible thought-leaders. Positive Twitter mentions serve much the same purpose.

Once again, this may be an area essential to your own KPIs, but it requires analysis and refinement before deployment.

Sales Lead Quality

Content-oriented marketing initiatives crafted to engage and educate a target audience are the most effective at driving "high value leads most likely to convert to sales" (Lenskold Group/emedia Lead Generation Marketing ROI study, 2010).

Yet to implement sales-lead quality as a metric, you must first define a "quality lead." Eloqua has done so by parsing out VP and above titles from its average site visitor and content consumer. Bear in mind, however, that this depends on the type of offering and sales cycle. It's hard to define a "quality lead" for toothpaste, because everyone buys it. In large enterprises, a VP may not be as important a qualifier as someone from Procurement. Alternatively, a high-quality lead may be someone who's watched an online demo and downloaded a whitepaper prior to getting in touch.

By all means, measure sales lead quality. But before you do, ensure you can define and identify it!

Search and Social Media Ranking/Visibility

Increased search awareness, as discussed in an earlier chapter, is often a primary goal of content marketing. It's not just getting the company or product name to rank high in organic search results; it's also ranking for the relevant keywords and phrases searchers use to find what you're offering—at all stages of the sales and lead development cycle. Web analytics gauge this. So do services such as Alexa.com and Compete.com, which benchmark search terms for you as well as competitors.

Boosting search engine optimization (SEO) ranking is more than mere visibility, however. Judiciously optimizing for the right keywords connects you to the right visitors who are most likely to engage with content and, ultimately, to convert.

Similarly, social media visibility boosts search rankings and can increase awareness, buzz, branding, and other key metrics around a brand, product, or service.

Conclusion

An attractive aspect of content marketing to many is the fact that it's a highly creative, right-brained discipline. Content marketers get to tell stories, use images, produce videos, play wordsmith, and be editors. Yet all that creativity must be governed by discipline, measurement, and a strong degree of precision. Choosing what metrics matter, why, and how to actually go about measuring them is just as critical as the creative element of content marketing.

Index